Table of Cont

A threatened rural idyll?

Informal social control, exclusion and the resistance to change in the English Countryside

Nathan Aaron Kerrigan

Centre for Advances in Behavioural Science,
Coventry University, UK

Series in Sociology

www.vernonpress.com

In the Americas:
Vernon Press
1000 N West Street,
Suite 1200, Wilmington,
Delaware 19801
United States

In the rest of the world:
Vernon Press
C/Sancti Espiritu 17,
Malaga, 29006
Spain

Series in Sociology

Library of Congress Control Number: 2018944699

ISBN: 978-1-62273-418-4

List of Figures

List of Tables

For Grampy, and Grandma

"You toiled away and at the end of the day you both can look back on a life well played".

Chapter 1

Introduction:
Framing the parameters of the book

The general consensus amongst social scientists is that we are living in a turbulent world undergoing a major restructuring. Globalisation has had an impact on social life at an unprecedented level. Places are becoming tied together by the compression of time-space through developments in technological communications, cheap air travel and multiculture (Giddens, 1991; Massey, 1994; Neal 2009). While the increased connectivity of globalisation has had some positive impact on society, it has not, as some policymakers and politicians have maintained, subsumed or diminished the idea of nation states or ushered in a monolithic, global culture. In many ways, it has done the opposite as when perceptions of uncertainty and change are acute people begin to look for ways in which to latch onto identity to protect who they are and maintain a sense of ontological security.

Britain has not escaped from this global turbulence, the most striking manifestation of which has been Brexit. On 23 June 2016, the British public voted to leave the EU by 52–48 percent. Goodwin and Heath (2016) have claimed that the relatively unexpected victory of Brexit was driven by the same processes which led United Kingdom Independence Party (UKIP) being voted into the European Parliament in 2014 and gain political footing during the 2015 UK General Election. That is, the vote for Brexit was perceived to be delivered by those *'left behind'* by globalisation - all those 'pensioners, low-skilled, less well-educated blue-collar workers and citizens who have been pushed to the margins' (Goodwin and Heath, 2016: 13).

What was also evident within the discourses surrounding Brexit was the presence of narratives around external threats and internal dangers against whom Britain has often defined and defended itself including, most notably, racialised minorities and migrants (e.g., Habermas, 2016). And there was something about this racialisation of minorities and migrants exhibited in the discursive dimensions of the 'Leave' campaigns. For instance, within the discourses of *Vote Leave* – the official 'Leave' campaign of the Referendum led by senior Conservative MPs such as Boris Johnson and Michael Gove and a scattering of Labour MPs such as Kate Hoey and Frank Field –a narrative around a forward-looking 'Global Britain' was cast, one whereby leaving the EU Britain could once again secure trade agreements with other common-wealth nations (e.g., Australia, New Zealand) as well as emerging global econ-omies (e.g., China, India). However, this 'Global Britain' project was less about creating a forward-looking 'Global Britain' and more about invoking warm collective memories of a now lost world where Britain was the global hegemon of the world economy (Gilroy 2005). It was about reminding the British public of those glory days of economic, political and cultural superiori-ty, where everything from ships to spoons was marked with a *Made in Britain* stamp while failing to talk about the corrosive legacies of colonialism and racism, past and present. Likewise, the second campaign, *Leave.EU* – the unofficial 'Leave' campaign of the Referendum led by then UKIP leader Nigel Farage - employed a more insular, Powellite narrative of retreat from a global-ising world that is no longer recognisably 'British'. The rhetoric of *Leave.EU* constructed migrants as an economic and security threat to the British public. This argument was made most powerfully in the lead-in to the June 23 vote through *Leave. EU's* infamous *'Breaking Point'* poster, which pictured Middle Eastern refugees queuing at Europe's borders, with the subheading reading: 'We must break free of the EU and take back control.' This was a message of 'island retreat' (Winter 2016): that is, if Britons voted to leave they could suc-cessfully keep such people from entering the country. It was these representa-tions of racialised minorities and migrants which gave these visions traction and indeed Brexit vindication, amongst the British public, in which they care-fully activated long-standing racialised structures of feeling about immigra-tion and national belonging.

While there has been much political and scholarly debate concerning these issues of globalisation, protection of identity and the resistance to change at the national level, especially in relation to Brexit, little is known about its relational association with local contexts. One particular example of this is within the English countryside. Like national identity, rural identity appears to offer a set of shared bonds. Like national identity, rural identity has pre-modern and almost organic associations; and like national identity, rural identity can offer senses of ontological certainty and reassurance in the face of insecurity and change. Indeed, long-term residents of rural settlements are becoming overwhelmed by globalising forces, since these processes result in feelings of ontological insecurity that they are living in an unstable and uncer-tain world. Sarah Neal's (2009) book, *Rural Identities*, suggests these feelings are heightened when long-term residents of rural settlements feel the local rural identity of their area is threatened and at stake of erosion from wider social and spatial change and will extend efforts into actualising a sense of rural community to mitigate concerns of loss of identity.

This book, therefore, will take stock at these issues by highlighting how residents from a small but developing rural town in the south of England, particularly those of middle-class status and long standing in the town, perceived changes associated with globalisation, such as population growth, inappropriate building developments, and the influx of service industries, as a threat to the rural character of the place. The book will do this by exploring the community dynamics and socio-spatial organisation of daily life, enacted through informal social control, that were set out to protect the rural traditions inherent in the social and spatial landscape of the town and maintain the dominance of its largely white, middle class character to the exclusion of individuals and processes seen as representing more diverse values and opinions.

Why informal social control, exclusion & the resistance to change in the English countryside?

I began questioning the relationship between informal social control, exclusion, and the resistance to globalised social change in the English countryside in 2012 as part of my doctoral work. Sarah Neal and Julian Agyeman (2006a: 242) concluded in their edited collection, *The New Countryside? Ethnicity, nation and exclusion in contemporary rural Britain*, that rural social science research needs to go beyond the lens of hate crime victimisation when examining issues of exclusion and racism within the English countryside, and instead argued for what they called more 'broken narratives of the rural'. By this they meant that the global turbulences which impact the English countryside needed to be accounted for – that is, the countryside needed to be more widely acknowledged as an uncertain landscape, as a site of social struggle and cultural and social heterogeneity and, directly related to this heterogeneity, as an unsettled and 'threatened space' where the exclusion and racism of minority ethnic individuals is a product of wider actions and practices of the host rural community to protect and maintain their rural identity in light of the global turbulences happening in the English countryside. In short Neal and Agyman called for a richer understanding of what Neil Chakraborti and Jon Garland (2004) coined 'rural racism' in contemporary Britain.

Since Neal and Agyman's (2006a) call for broken narratives of rurality there has been a flurry of books (e.g., Askwith, 2007; Kingsnorth, 2007; 2011) and media debate (see, for example, The Independent 22 August 2013) about the impact of social change on the English countryside. At the heart of these books and media, discussions are expressions of anxiety as to a vanishing countryside. This anxiety is by no means a new one – as Raymond Williams (1979) observed nearly four decades ago – the worry of golden rurality that has, or is about to disappear irrevocably has always had a constant presence (e.g., Neal and Agyeman, 2006a). However, what is interesting is the timing around the resurgence of this 'threatened rural idyll' discourse. This debate has come at a time when, intensified by the continual background and not so background white noise of a 'crisis of multiculturalism' (Lewis and Neal, 2005; McLaughlin and Neal, 2007) and the ongoing uncertainty over Brexit, rurality and its dominant politicised position and meaning is increasingly fragile. Of course, the worries about an eroding rural identity should be written into the anxieties about loss of Britishness, reinforcing the global-local relationship between nation and countryside where global problems become rural issues. In other words, the countryside is a mirror which should be viewed as being in crisis and of which is a reflection of the (seeming) crisis of Britishness that led the British public voting in favour of leaving the EU.

The rise of the service industry has had a fundamental impact on agriculture and the dynamics of rural life in much of England and the wider UK. This is starkly apparent in even the briefest glances at statistics. For example, Benson (2005: 228) notes that while in 1939 there were 500,000 farms in Britain, there are now fewer than 191,000 farms left with an estimated three out of four jobs in British agriculture being lost since 1945. The extent to which the countryside has undergone systematic processes of economic restructuring is also reflected in the shift from the 1950s when 'over a third (34.6 percent) of the "rural population" of Britain was estimated to be dependent on agriculture for its income. By 1970 the proportion had fallen to 24.3 percent, by 1990 to 19.6 percent and by 2000 to 16.8 percent' (Woods, 2005: 15). Even the most recent figure shows a continued and rapid decline in the agricultural base of rural economies – according to the Commission for Rural Communities (2012: 2) 'agriculture accounts for no more than 2.8% of employment in rural areas'. This decline of agriculture has been accompanied by an increase in service industries 'opening up' on rural High Streets. Businesses like *Costa Coffee* and *Waitrose* now occupy rural High Streets and sit alongside local, independent retailers, and this is of concern for those who would identify as longer-standing residents of rural areas because there is a tendency to see and a preconception of bigger businesses coming in and eroding local identity and character, regardless of who or what is affected, in the conquest of making monetary gains (see Chapter 3 for more details).

There is, of course, a social recursiveness to these changes of which these economic shifts are an interactive part. Counter urbanisation and the flow of urban to rural migration (as well as global migrations) reflect, in part, imagined rural idylls that need protecting and to be in and ensure the security of. Of course, rural migration and changes to the social mix of the English countryside has had impact on and influences the changing nature of rural spaces and communities (e.g., greater service industry, housing expansion), but we must not forget changes to the English countryside would have happened gradually anyway as rural areas develop and expand as part of the globalised world (see Chapter 3). So, while there is no denying that the countryside is undergoing processes of major change and restructuring, I do think, however, it is more interesting, for this book, to focus on how long-term rural residents attempt to protect and maintain rural identity more representative of an *'rural idyll'* than *'rural crisis'* (see Table 1.1) to the exclusion of diverse processes and individuals than it is to focus on the broader impact and dynamics globalised social change has had on rural England.

Table 1.1 – Rural Idyll versus Rural Crisis

Rural Idyll	Rural Crisis
Intact communities	Break down of communities
A sense of community	House prices and housing shortages
Safety and security	Closure of shops and social amenities
Neighbourliness and social care	
Small scale and local agricultural economies	A lack of neighbourliness and an absence of social care
Open spaces	Rural restructuring and the rise of agri-business
Privacy and solitude	
Proximity to nature and rural traditions	Commuting
Reaffirming Englishness and cultural security	Isolation
	Attacks and restrictions on rural practices and traditions
Timelessness	Loss of national identity and cultural insecurity
	Constant change

Taken from Sarah Neal's (2009) book 'Rural Identities'

Mapping out the key features of each discourse of rurality in this way demonstrates their connectedness rather than their separateness. While the idyll and crisis discourses of the contemporary English countryside are worked up as distinctively different by those long-term residents of rural communities – idyll as good, crisis as bad - it would appear as though they work in parallel to the other in which they continually bump into, collide with and co-constitute each other. It is notions of community and a shared social identity that in particular work as the socially based drivers in these conjoined discourses but these are also bound by and interact with notions of space. At one level this is a very obvious point to make. After all, the spatial context is where 'the social relations of the countryside' take place, and 'the countryside is all about real and imagined forms of social relations' (Neal, 2009: 5). But surprisingly, in many of the debates about rural spaces, their contestations and the processes and practices of social inclusion and exclusion, rural space itself is often uncommented on, taken as a given or as the forgotten guest at a party (see Bell and Newby 1979; Cohen 1982 for example). This splitting between the social and spatial worlds produces a focus on the former, with the latter providing the mere context in which the dramas of the social are carried out.

What this book does, therefore, is engage with both the sociality and spatiality of the English countryside. It may seem commonsensical but by incorporating rural space directly into the worries about all that is being lost and damaged within their 'threatened rural idyll' discourse I attempt to illustrate how those long-term rural residents with greatest vested interests create and draw upon the spatial landscapes of the English countryside in constructing a sense of rural identity and how this construction of rural identity and the desire to protect and maintain it from wider globalised social change gets written into experiences of exclusion and racism for minority ethnic individuals. What seems important to me is to ask in this context how does this structurated construction of rurality give rise to particular ways of doing and being rural? And how and at what moments does this structured construction of rurality get drawn upon and invested in to enact informal social control in everyday social routines, practices, and actions to resist globalised social change and the extent to which this excludes and racialises minority ethnic individuals from belonging?

In 1992 Chris Philo's paper, *Neglected Rural Geographies*, called for rural social scientists to rethink the relationship between rurality and its marginalised and diverse populations. This seminal paper has since helped reshape the theoretical and empirical directions of rural studies over the 1990s and 2000s (Cloke and Little, 1997). In their response to Philo, however, Murdoch and Pratt (1994: 85) warned against any simplistic refocusing of the analytical gaze on 'hidden others' in rural spaces and posed the question 'should we not attempt to reveal the ways of the powerful, exploring the means by which they make and sustain their domination?' With this debate in mind I am particularly interested in understanding how long-term residents of English rural communities attempt to sustain the dominance of their mainly white, middle-class character in light of the big changes happening globally and how their actions/routines give rise to unintended exclusionary consequences towards individuals and processes seen as representing a more diverse set of values and opinions. I use the term, *long-term residents*, to describe those rural populations who can appear to make a confident, dominant and a seemingly uncontested claim to rural belonging. My interest was in the ethnographic excavation of these rural community dynamics and processes enacted through informal social control: what were these controls and in what ways are they enacted? What are the tensions and nuances that arose from resisting globalisation and in what ways and in what spaces did exclusion and racism enter and shape these processes?

At the heart of this project, therefore, was the following research question: to what extent does informal social control have exclusionary and racist consequences in maintaining and protecting the rural identity of the English countryside? To answer this specific research question, an ethnographic study was conducted from September 2013-November 2014 in a small English rural town that I have called Brickington. Through employing semi-structured interviews, direct observations and participant observations, the aim was to examine community dynamics and the socio-spatial organisation of daily life, enacted through routines and engagement with specific local events. As is the usual practice of ethnography, Brickington, the names of residents, places, and businesses identified in this book have been given pseudonyms to hide their true identity. However, while there is no scope in this introductory chapter to provide a rigorous breakdown of the methodology adopted for the study I do discuss – in greater depth - the details of the research project and setting (including data collection methods used) and methodological issues arising from the project elsewhere in this book (see Methodological Appendix, and Chapter 5) to contextualise the findings discussed at various points in the chapters below. It is the structure of the book and the focus of its chapters that I now outline.

How this book is organised

Working across seven substantial chapters, this book begins in Chapter Two by addressing the global context surrounding concepts of globalisation, identity, and resistance to change. This chapter will suggest that British national identity has always been and will continue to be a hybridised imagined and 'real' space of highly diverse and competing demands, desires, anxieties, claims, commodifications, and consumptions. The chapter is centred around how certain groups of citizens – those of white, longer-standing British residence – construct and draw upon idealised narratives of Britishness to provide ontological security in a world of globalised change which brings with it uncertainty: uncertainty of uncontrollable migrations and uncertainty of nationhood. The chapter is particularly concerned with how such perceived threat produced processes of social and cultural exclusion within narratives of protecting British national identity, and how Brexit was used to anchor British national identity and resist change in an insecure, global world.

Directly developing the themes of the previous chapter, Chapter Three focuses on the way the debates around British national identity, globalisation, and resistance to change are reproduced in very localised ways by examining the enduring appeal of the concept rural community. It will do this by tracking the ways in which the notion of 'community' has been approached in the sociological, criminological and geographical literature, and by exploring the tangential but connected discourses of 'rural communities'. The chapter will highlight that despite the impact and influence of globalised social change which has produced ontological insecurity, it is the enduring appeal of the countryside and the ontological securities from which it provides in a global social world, that people seek to maintain ideas and notions of 'problem-free' everyday informal social relations and identity construction.

Chapter 4 continues to build upon the themes developed in Chapters 2 and 3 and considers how informal social control is enacted to protect identity against social change, and the influence informal social control has on precipitating exclusion and racism. The chapter will begin by contextualising the ways in which informal social control has been approached within the Chicago School and environmental criminology. Borrowing from the sociological literature, this chapter refocuses the theoretical development of informal social control beyond the study of crime management by arguing that the enactment of informal social control can be explored in a wider context of identity protection and maintenance. The latter part of this chapter will go on to contextualise the unanticipated consequences of informal social control. Here, the chapter will critique the concept of social exclusion as a means of simply explaining the feelings and experiences of those outside of the dominant social group. Social exclusion is also an expression of complex interrelationship of vested interests, common identity and shared values of the dominant social group which creates boundaries around who can and cannot belong within a specific context. One of the social harms that may arise from social exclusion is racism. The chapter will define racism in this context as a structural process, derived unwittingly from community action and practices to maintain and protect rural identity in which while, all newcomers are excluded based on operating outside of the boundary of a particular identity; minority ethnic individuals are doubly excluded, and racialised, because of their perceived visible differences.

Chapter 5 empirically develops the issues of rural community and social change raised in Chapter 3. The chapter examines the local changes occurring in Brickington, which are viewed as a threat to the local rural identity of the place. Socio-spatial organisation and power are explored by focussing on the carnival in the local area in which long-term residents used to maintain their specific rural identity against the backdrop of social change. The symbolic imagery of the procession reinforced the rural and picturesque nature of the place. However, this was contingent on longer-term residents with the greatest material and emotional investment in the area who constructed such imagery during the procession.

Chapter 6 develops the socio-spatial factors discussed in the preceding chapter and their impact on informal social control. The first part of this chapter will draw on observational data to identify how structural, ideological and cultural controls were enacted passively to reinforce the rural identity of Brickington. The second part will then examine the enactment of 'active' community controls that sought to prevent the social and physical changes happening in the town.

Chapter 7 turns to the unanticipated consequences of informal social control. The chapter starts by highlighting that while there was an obvious discourse around the erosion of the locality's specific rural character, community routines and action was less attributable to fears of the erosion of rural identity and character, but more to the structural processes of resisting newcomers. The chapter goes on to maintain that this created an exclusive and exclusionary community based on vested interests, common social identity and shared values among those residents with middle-class status and longer-standing in the town. Lastly, the chapter details the experience of those minority ethnic residents in the locality to unpick the racist consequences of informal social control.

Chapter 8 brings together the issues discussed in previous chapters by returning to the discourses around 'rural community under threat' and the argument that globalisation has eroded rural community as much as it has facilitated its continuity. This chapter illustrates how narratives about social change (e.g., urbanisation, migration, neoliberal expansionism, the internet), loss of rural identity and the corresponding rise of ontological insecurity in rural communities (while tangential to) go together with the narratives around the reassertion of rural identity which needs protecting from social change and the exclusionary consequences of community actions and routines which mark out rurality as a site of security and reassurance within a turbulent, insecure world. It is these tangential but nevertheless connected discourses that the first part of this chapter takes stock of. Moreover, Chapter 8 also examines the central significances of the book through discussing the global-local relationship between Brexit and rurality, as well as the myth of the UK's 'Shared Society' agenda. Lastly, this chapter will explore the possible ways in which the data explored, and discussions had throughout this book can have 'real world' policy implications, especially as Britain heads towards a post-Brexit future.

Chapter 2

Turbulent and Mighty Country:
Globalisation, British nationhood & Brexit

Introduction

What is it meant by Britishness? How can the relationship between the social, the cultural, ethnicity and indeed space be understood as British? In what ways is each contingent and how does each constitute the other to construct Britishness? Is Britishness solely an ethnic, social and culturally-based concept? What threatens and dislocates what it means to be British in a globalising world? It is these kinds of questions which this chapter attempts to think through, but in order to tease out the answers we must first ask ourselves, what is 'home'?

Les Back (2007) reminds us that the concept of 'home' has very different associations. Citing John Berger, Back emphasises the diverse meanings of home, encompassing domestic, morality, property and family and even extends out to notions of homeland, nationhood and countless forms of patriotism, nationalism, and jingoism. But, as Back (2007: 69) also remind us, 'there is an antecedent meaning…home is the centre of the world – not in a geographical, but an ontological sense…the place from which the world can be founded'. It is these multidimensional meanings of home, and by association, security that lie in Michael Kenny's (2014) suggestion that British nationhood tends to have a physical, historical and emotional focus at its core which gets called upon in times of crisis and change as to protect and defend what it means to be British within the twenty-first century, which is marked by a range of risks, threats, and dangers (Giddens, 2013).

In a roundabout way then I have begun to describe the task this chapter will set itself – understanding the processes whereby Britishness is constructed; the extent to which it has been disrupted by globalising forces (e.g., greater geopolitical integration, continuous migrations and increasing individualism) and how British nationhood has been mobilised in light of these wider globalised changes as a way of protecting and securing a sense of ontological security. Divided into three broad sections the first section of this chapter addresses some of the thinking of what constitutes Britishness. The second section focuses on the turbulent nature of Britishness in the face of a changing world, and the third section presents Brexit as a national response that pushed back against such wider changes happening globally as a way of securing British nationhood and what it means to be 'home'.

Conceptualising British nationhood: formations of a social, cultural and ethnic identity

I began this chapter by proposing questions about what we recognise and know as being British and what provides it with a sense of 'home', familiarity and comfort – e.g., processes of confirming the ontological security of the nation. Through cultural symbols and signs (e.g., red telephone boxes, black taxi cabs, cream teas and so on) perceptions of British nationhood are often mobilised as to confirm a type of social and ethnic identity and sense of belonging. In a range of daily, political, policy and social science contexts, nationhood is overwhelmingly associated with and used to define the cultural content and practices of the 'included' or majoritised populations rather than minoritised ones. Nationhood can be an acceptable longhand for the cultural 'us' as opposed to 'them'. In this way, the majoritised population becomes *de-ethnicised* and takes on the status as 'the norm' against which all other cultures are compared and explicitly 'othered'. This conceptualisation of nationhood as something rooted in the social and ethnic identification of a majoritised population is supported by Mac an Ghail's (1999: 41) observation that nationhood is an 'ethnicity that is not named as such' and therefore needs to be scrutinised. But despite a stream of books from the late-1990s/early-2000s (e.g., Paxman, 1998; Scruton, 2000), these do not speak to Mac an Ghail's (1999: 41) call for scrutiny on an 'ethnicity that is not named as such' but rather concentrate on an encroaching unease about the meaning of and changes in Britishness, or rather Englishness, and crises about, as Vron Ware (2007: 2) describes it, 'national identity and identity of the nation'. As I write this chapter, I am thinking about what it is to be British. Is it the Edwardian and Victorian architecture? Is it the white cliffs of Dover? Is it the real cask ales and stout? Is it the red telephone boxes, black taxi cabs, and afternoon teas? Indeed, these cultural symbols loaded with familiarity and fantasy are what we conjure up and allude to when we think about the British nation-state and British national identity, a social, cultural, political and ethnic territory as much as a geographical one.

Neal (2009) in her book, *Rural Identities,* maintains that the co-constituted relationship between national identity and ethnic identity is an unsurprising one. Nations draw heavily on ideas of shared culture, kinship, history and ethnic identity is not without its geographical context - ethnicity relies on having ties to real and imagined homelands. Nevertheless, these categories are not completely collapsible into each other and such delineations are not easily drawn and marked out in social relations. Each may borrow from itself to reinforce the other. Each works with notions of being natural and a given rather than being assembled and constructed. The political/cultural distinction has been used to establish discourses of a political hegemony – national identity has been one that has been used to describe majoritised populations whereas ethnicity has been mobilised to describe minoritised, subordinated populations, for example. Billig (2002) advocates that British nationhood has received the most attention in its extreme and 'thickly' politicised form. Billig's argument, of which as Neal (2009) claims ethnicity can be an extension, is that it is important to understand the ways in which British nationhood can operate in everyday and banal ways and so continually reminds us and allows us to interpret our own sense of national identity and what it means to be Britishness.

The work of Bhattacharyya (1999: 81) extends this line of reference by denoting how identities face similar problems and challenges and that identities are mostly 'marked out for those in some way that inhabit the margins of society. The powerful (all those infamous straight white middle class privileged and able-bodied men) seem to have hardly any identity at all'. It is interesting that Bhattacharyya lists whiteness here because studies of whiteness (see, for instance, Frankenberg, 1993) have too laboured to excavate and define the meanings of social practices of whiteness away from the obvious sites of white supremacy politics. The categories of national identity, whiteness, and ethnicity share the same challenges when mapped onto the cartographies of powerfulness. All of these are categories that are proximate and relational. They melt into and sustain each other. It is no surprise therefore that British nationhood works in the same way – while minoritised ethnicities are continuously flagged and marked out as distinct and separate, the majoritised British national identity works as unremarkable and ubiquitous and in this way presents itself as normative and thereby dominant. British nationhood is not seen as ethnic, but rather a cultural given, as culturally universalist. In this way Bangla dancing is ethnic but Morris dancing not. Jalebi is ethnic but Cornish pasties not.

These are rather light-hearted examples of course, but they do work to starkly illustrate the 'us' and 'them' formations and processes of the ethnic identification of British nationhood. In this context, Britishness is not nationalistic but ethnic instead. However, I am a little tentative in making claims like Britishness is an ethnic identity as it feels as though I am skirting rather close to concretising and privileging the cultural hegemony of British nationhood and its associated, and spurious claims to cultural superiority which have long been part of colonialism that continue to inform and inflect many contemporary understandings of Britishness.

Nonetheless, what I am suggesting is that British nationhood, for the purposes of this book, would be better understood through the interactions of social relations, culture and ethnicity; and more specifically, through cultural differences, and socio-cultural and socio-spatial practices. Barth (1969: 15) has denoted nationhood as 'the social organisation of cultural signifiers' and Geertz (1973: 63) as 'the world of personal identity collectively ratified and publicly expressed'. Stressing the connectivity between the external social environment and people's individual lifeworlds, Jenkins (1999) identifies four key elements in a very usual base model for understanding nationhood:

- Nationhood is about social and cultural signification.

- Although nationhood is centrally concerned with culture, it has its roots in and is an outcome of social interaction.

- Nationhood is no more fixed or unchanging as the culture of which it is a component of.

- Nationhood is a social and ethnic identity which is both collectively and individually externalised in social interaction and internalised in personal self-awareness.

Jenkins' (1999) model rightly places emphasis on the centrality of the social in the construction of nationhood but also on the inherent instabilities in ethnic identification. But what Jenkins's model does not pay heed to is the role that emotion plays into what Fenton (1999: 92) calls 'the intensity of ethnic identification and sentiment of the nation'. The inclusion of emotion into the already over-packed recipe of nationhood is important. Not only is it a liable category but nationhood has a history in academic study and the wider social world as a concept rooted in individualised emotive, personal connections to place. In fact, the actual roots of the term nationhood go back to older related usages – most notably the Greek word *ethnos* – which Hutchinson and Smith (1996) note was used to refer to a band of friends, a tribe, societies and nations. The recent focusing and ascendancy of British nationhood in the lead up to and following the 2016 EU Referendum in mainstream every day and political discourses has been to maintain and confirm ontological security against the perceived risks and threats that globalisation throws up. But before we can explore the impact and consequences globalisation has had on British nationhood, I want to spend a little longer mapping out what gives Britishness its social, cultural and ethnic identification. To do this, we must now turn to the anthropological concept of *primordialism*.

British nationhood: importance of the primordial

The role of the primordial within formations of nationhood has been an extended debate within anthropology and sociology (Geertz, 1973; Barth, 1969; Banton, 1983; Rex and Mason 1986; Jenkins, 1997; Fenton, 1999). The primordial refers to an idea of a fixed and unchanging social and ethnic identity that is rooted in the notions of kinship, place, language, culture, and history – in its most basic conceptualisation, it is understood as a 'born and bred' identity. While the focus of the primordial has been contrasted with the situational and instrumental arguments that nationhood is a socio-political product that is fluid and context specific, Jenkins (1999) has maintained that the polarity between these and their associated theorists, Geertz (1973) and Barth (1969), has been overstated. Jenkins asserts that Geertz recognised the importance of culture and its ability to change nationhood over space and time, and Barth acknowledged that the ethnic formations of nationhood contain stability to them which means that the ethnic identities associated with and attached to particular nationhoods may change not that they inevitability do. Wallman (1986: 230) also argues that Barth's well-known metaphor of nationhood being a 'vessel' of (and for) boundary construction which is sometimes empty and sometimes full but 'always there' is suggestive of the primordial. There is a general consensus within the social sciences – based on theoretical argument and ethnographic research – that the 'pure' primordial view of nationhood is inaccurate and speaks mostly to common sense understandings of national identity. As Bhattacharyya (1999: 81, emphasis added) argues, we have moved away from ideas of 'nationhood as a negative determination – instead of seeing a fixed (and often atrocious) legacy which you inhabit, British nationhood can be understood as a *strategic performance*: something which is staged in everyday life according to circumstances, and using a variety of repertoires that might include the 'traditional' as well as the influences of the new context'.

However, what is relevant to my discussions is the extent to which notions of the primordial dominate the conceptualisations of British national identity. This reflects a duality of the internalised life worlds of the individual and the collective, public social world through which nationhood/national identity is subscribed to. In other words, because nationhood partially works through attachments and affections and familiarities and recognition, then the emotional should be incorporated into considerations of the ways in which national identity is performed and mobilised. Again, Jenkins (1997: 97) makes the important observation that we 'need to acknowledge affect and emotion in our considerations of nationhood [...] but there is, there must be said no necessary contradiction instrumental manipulation on the one hand and sentiment, on the other. They may actually go hand in hand'.

It is precisely nationhood's ability to work in and through emotional regis-
ters which means the idea of the primordial needs to be focussed on in the
examination of processes of formation of national identity. There is, for example, a sense of the primordial in Williams' (1979: 106) description of his
relationship to the place where he grew up and the notion of nationhood, of
home: 'The only landscape I ever see, in dreams, is the Black Mountain village
in which I was born. When I go back...I feel a recovery of a particular kind of
life...and inescapable identity...a positive connection.'

Reading through the account of Williams' (1979) bonds with the place he
grew up in illustrates Urry's (2002: 77) observation that geographical attachments can be deeply embedded between people and the places in which they
reside and the ways in which emotions 'are intimately tied to places'. Therefore the primordial dimension of nationhood cannot be discounted as it reflects two similar key aspects of social and ethnic identities. First, as I discussed above, the personal and the emotional are particularly profound and
so lend themselves to being experienced and viewed through the optic of the
primordial – these are the emotions that make us feel un/comfortable and
in/secure. It can be difficult to express and articulate emotions and the basis
and reasons for them, so they tend to stay at that primordially 'instinctive'
level (Bondi *et al.,* 2005).

Second, the foregrounding of the primordial gives nationhood its inherited,
passed on, born into, *given* character. In the same way 'race science' draws
heavily on biological discourses as a social process, representations of nationhood as primordial allows the cultural and social components that make
up a national identity to become naturalised. However, this idea and representation of emotion of attachment as being *beyond* the social is troubling.
While I acknowledge the establishment of effective relationships with the
landscapes in which we are familiar does have a structural, instinctively primordial element to it, they are not completely without an element of the social, which is the second part of the construction of nationhood process that
we all engage in to feel at ease and comfortable. Within a globalised world,
there is no requirement to have been born in a country or have generational
ties back into a nationalised past to develop a sense of home, belonging and
place of affection. Instead, nationhood is constructed from and out of people's *elective belongings.* As Savage *et al.* (2005: 207) put it, elective belonging
is a process whereby people move to a place and construct home. In other
words, belonging is rooted in the biographical and the decisions people make
to move to a particular place and the connection they draw between themselves and their wider spatial environment. Within this context, nationhood
can be interpreted as a 'duality of structure' (Giddens, 1984). Nationhood is
enacted in place (e.g., within places in Britain) which provides a structured

context for individuals to emphasise the primordial aspects of Britishness (e.g., red telephone boxes, Yorkshire terriers, pasties and so on) that become representational of what it means to be British. Such personal connections, in turn, reinforce the primordially structural representations that infer senses of Britishness.

It is the *elective* part of Savage *et al.'s* (2005) concept that is interesting as it implies that nationhood is not inherently primordial but rather gets assembled in a way that looks primordial through people's interaction with and influence of the wider social world. It is possible to see, therefore, the primordialism of British nationhood being continually folded into discourses about the perilously threatened nature of Britishness in light of the big global challenges happening in the world. It is these issues and problems which this chapter now turns to.

<h2 style="text-align:center">Turbulent and mighty country:
Britain & unstable nationhood in a globalised world?</h2>

The world in which we inhabit today is much different to the one envisioned during the Enlightenment. Enlightenment philosophers suggested the more we get to know about the world through the advance of science and technology, and the more we get to know about ourselves and our histories the more we can master the world, control the world and control our fate as human beings. This enlightenment view, although with some simplification suggested that such developments would lead to a more predictable and orderly world. However, if you look at the human experience today within the twenty-first century, the world does not look like this. The world as it is today does not look like a tightly ordered, rationally controlled world. Rather, it looks almost like the opposite, a world that is spinning out of control; a sort of 'runaway world' (Giddens 2000). A world marked by fractionalisation, by dislocation, and by a generalised feeling of uncertainty. This is because processes of globalisation have tied places together by time-space distanciation as a result of the internet revolution, continuous migrations and the dispersal of multilateral power (Giddens, 1984; Massey, 1994; Neal, 2009). This is perhaps best summed up by Bauman (2000: 11): 'the advent of cellular telephones may well serve as a symbolic "last blow" delivered to the dependency on space; and so, consequentially, the distance and exoticism of faraway lands become immediately accessible'.

Anthony Giddens in a series of public lectures in 2014 declared that this global age in which we currently live is like no other epoch come before it. This is not to say the world of today is completely different, it does indeed have continuities with previous civilisations; but rather, with the advent of globalisation and technological communication people's daily interactions and how we engage socially is not like any other civilisation in human history. For instance, we can now talk to individuals and be part of a community the other side of the world without having to leave the comfort of our home. Giddens in these lectures referred to this era as 'living off the edge of history' and by this, he means that society has developed so far and so quickly we cannot accurately predict or determine the future.

These processes of globalisation and the development of technological communication, where locales and nations are becoming disembedded from their local and national contexts and rearticulated across wide time-space distances, has had an impact on British nationhood. We can see this in the worries of commentators like Kingsnorth (2007: 238) who argues that globalisation has caused a sense of endangerment to the cultural, national, social and ethnic identification of Britishness – 'The British, perhaps uniquely among European nations, are becoming a de-cultured people'. Similarly, this sense of engenderment was also there in Scruton's (2000: 246) account of a crisis in identity brought about by globalised social change and how the conceptual wholeness of place enables stability and reassurance, 'when your fundamental loyalty is to a place, and its *genius loci*, globalisation and the loss of sovereignty bring crisis of identity. The land loses its history and its personal face […] it has induced in the British that they are actually living nowhere'.

This sense of unease and uncertainty and the associated risks that come from living within a globalised world have caused a sombre and generally more fearful and worrisome mood about the future of Britishness. As processes of globalisation have made possible the 'opening up' of Britain, this has facilitated the growth of more diverse populations, thus allowing a vast range of disparate identities to make up and construct what we know to be contemporary British life (Neal, 2009). Moreover, the rise of neoliberalism and gentrification has exacerbated the separation of the individual from wider society; creating further division and atomisation; divisions between rich and poor; the north and south; a division between elite politicians and the wider public; between experts and non-experts. Consequentially, British nationhood has become more representative of distrust, aggression, and misanthropy than one of collective pride and identity.

Although there is a general perception that uncertainty and change has destabilised British nationhood and has resulted in a greater sense of threat, insecurity and danger towards Britishness (Young, 2007), contemporary British society is one bounded by *high risks, high opportunities* (Giddens, 2013: 5); simply put, as globalisation erodes nationhood so too does it facilitate its continuity. Individuals in times of uncertainty call upon national identity as it appears to offer the shared bonds and values of nations that preceded the current global and political turbulence. We can see this in the way Bell (1975, cited in Hutchinson and Smith, 1996: 144) denotes the importance of nation-hood in the face of globalised change as it has the ability to 'combine interests with an effective tie' and prescribe a set of 'tangible common identifica-tions…in language, in food, music, names…when other social roles become more abstract and impersonal' in order to claim the place.

In the four decades that have passed since Bell (1975, cited in Hutchinson and Smith, 1996) made this observation the salience of British nationhood has become even more marked, and the processes of globalisation have in part shaped this. On 23rd June 2016, the British public decided to vote to leave the European Union. However, the decision to and sentiment around the vote for what is most commonly referred to as *'Brexit'* was not just a vote against the European Union, but a vote against cosmopolitan London, globalisation, and multiculturalism (Calhoun, 2016). It was a vote against cosmopolitan elites who the public perceived to be 'opening up' Britain through the en-dorsement of a 'global, corporate multiculture' (Neal, 2009) by keeping Britain a member of the EU. It was also a vote for a nostalgic past (Gilroy 2005), a reactionary social response to the global uncertainties (e.g., immigration, terrorism, bureaucracy and big government) of which this 'global era' has thrown up as to maintain a sense of security and national identity.

Despite the growing precariousness of British nationhood in light of ever-increasing and homogenising global connectivities this has by no means facil-itated the diminution or erosion of Britishness. Rather, it has aided its conti-nuity as people begin to look for ways in which to latch onto nationality to maintain and protect a sense of identity. We saw this in the lead up to the 2016 EU Referendum. The platform of the 'Leave' campaigns was one hinged on maintaining and protecting national identity and interests. There was a perception amongst 'Leave' campaigners that the EU was too imposing and that being part of the EU weakened British national identity and its place as a global powerhouse. There was also a perception that being part of the EU brought with it greater uncertainty: uncertainties of uncontrollable migra-tions and uncertainties of increased terrorist activity. For the 'Leave' cam-paigners, therefore, the idea of 'Brexit' was about having greater security by reasserting control over British borders and claiming back sovereignty from the EU by leaving the single market as to reinstate a perceived *past greatness* (Gilroy, 2005) of the UK.

While the reassertion and valorising of British nationhood is not problemat-ic, it does become so when it is conceived of as a defensive partnership be-tween place, culture, and ethnicity. In fact, it was the notion of the reassertion of Britishness as a defensive identity that ran through the 'Leave' campaigns in the lead up to and during the 2016 EU Referendum. This idea of Britishness as a defensive identity forces my hand to perform a contextualisation of the defensiveness of British nationhood before moving my argument forwards in exploring how Brexit was an act of controlling and securing the nation. This is important because the notion of defensive identities requires analysis because of the ways in which the idea has been drawn upon in explaining why Brexit happened (see for instance the work of Outhwaite, 2017).

Britishness as a defensive identity

I maintained earlier in this chapter that British nationhood was based on elective belonging, that Britishness was given its primordial feel through the interaction some individuals (normally those white, middle-class long-term citizens) have with the country's wider spatial environment and that this interaction was dependent on the persons' emotional and psychological attachment to Britishness. Although it is possible to see using this concept a certain level of openness within British nationhood this is largely uneven and time and context specific and subject to revision and amnesias (see, for example, Hall, 1992; Gilroy, 1987; 2004; Ware, 2007).

Alongside this unpredictable openness, there tends to be an accompanying conditionality in terms of an attachment to place and enabling and facilitating routes of belonging and this is particularly acute to the notion of Britishness. As I will go on and discuss in more detail in Chapter 4, inclusion is contingent on processes of informal social control of the dominant group (e.g., those white, middle-class long-term citizens) who regulate the behaviours of newcomer groups (particularly minority ethnic newcomers) as to make sure they internalise and externally portray the required behaviours of the nation as to maintain, protect and secure a sense of British national identity. Therefore, while it is worked up as though newcomers can be included into British nationhood and stake claims of belonging to the nation, they can only do so if they meet the requirements of sameness, 'fitting in' and conditionality on part of what it means to be British. Britishness in this context holds the potential for openness, cultural change, and border crossings but, as Chapter 4 makes claim, there are also other exclusionary and racialised demands and anxieties which continually drag at these transformative possibilities.

It is these processes of informal social control (see Chapter 4 for a detailed discussion) that connect to the defensive policing of the ways in which British nationhood gets defined and reflected in the melancholic emphasis on the (selective) past in the threatened Britain narrative. Wallman (1986: 230) argues that while the most common 'items' to be mobilised in terms of British nationhood are 'language, history, territory, and economic considerations' there is a limitless range of things that can be called upon to delineate a national boundary marked by social, cultural and ethnic identifications. This is an important point in relation to British nationhood, as the following passage from Kingsnorth (2007: 283) illustrates - 'we can't sing our own folk songs or increasingly, cook our own national foods. We don't know what grows in our local area. We sneer at Morris dancers as we sip our skinny lattes. We are cut off from who we are and where we have come from' – because it is the bundling of individualised sense-making with the wider spatial environment that provides British nationhood with its primordial feel and which get filtered into the 'de-cultured' and loss discourse position of 'threatened Britishness'. My suggestion as to why this might be is simple and follows the arguments made by Neal (2009). As threats of globalisation encroach and perceptionally erode what it means to be British, people look to the nation and place emphasis on specific British national symbols to anchor their identity and assert identification, belonging and security in an uncertain, in-flux world. Consequentially these symbols, such as ideas of green lands, food, passing generations and certain socio-cultural practices (e.g., going down the pub), when connected to people's corporeal senses they become how and what we feel and see as a visceral experience of Britishness that needs protecting.

This process of assembling identity that draws on convergences between people's sense-making and the wider spatial environment is one which I examine in more detail in relation to local rural community life and the enactment of informal social control which seeks to maintain and protect local rural identity from a globalised social change in Chapters 5 and 6. For now, I want to consider an older account in which this process is very clearly captured in terms of Britishness. Philip Wright (2008: 82) quotes from Stanley Baldwin's many well-known descriptions of Britishness being the sound of the 'hammer on anvil in the country smithy', 'the sight of the plough team coming over the brow of a hill', and 'the smell of wood-smoke coming up in an autumn evening'. According to Baldwin these are all the things which 'strike down into the very depths of our nature and touch chords that go back to the beginning of time […] these are the things that make Britain and I grieve for it that they are not childish inheritance of the majority of people today in our country' (cited in Wright, 2008: 82).

These extracts which were written in 1926 are striking not only because they closely resemble the unease and worries of contemporary writers such as Kingsnorth (2007) and Scruton (2000) but because of the explicitly primordially framed connections between sense, self, sociality, culture, ethnicity, and nation that Baldwin's account sets up. As Wright (2008: 83) maintains in relation to Baldwin's work – although it is equally applicable to the more recent works I have been discussing in this book – there is an 'interpretative stress on the senses, on the experiences of meaning which are vitally incommunicable and indefinable' which contrasts sharply with how clear and important 'the sense of threat is to be in the definition of the nation'. In many ways, this is why globalisation and the development of technological communication that have taken place in Britain since the last quarter of the twentieth century and beginning of the twenty-first century have worked to galvanise and reshape the ways in which British nationhood is so politically contested (Giddens, 2002). It is impossible to see the form and turbulence of these processes of globalisation and technological change as separate from notions of threat.

However, in arguing that nationhood is mobilised, to use Barth's (1969) term, as a 'vessel' or container of social, cultural and ethnic meaning I want to stress it lends Britishness with what Wright (2008) describes as 'vagueness'. It is, in some ways, this vagueness and the fleeting, ephemeral features of definitions of Britishness that are significant. In his discussion of the work of interwar writers and poets Wright (2008: 109) argues that even colours become crucial in this process of assembling British nationhood, with 'green becoming the very grounds of an England of the mind' and 'the names – of villages, plants, landmarks, birds, stones and the accoutrements of British life [...] which aren't used to describe a world so much as to anxiously conjure one up'. While I do not want to overstate my suggestion here what I think can be read in Wight's account of the defensiveness nature of Britishness is the ephemerality of symbolism, and it is this that supposedly marked Britishness out as threatened in the lead up to and during the 2016 EU Referendum.

Brexit:
the unfinished process of controlling and securing the nation

As I have alluded to in previous sections of this chapter, there is clearly space to see Brexit and the 2016 EU referendum as a process of securing and controlling British nationhood for two reasons. Firstly, there was a discourse amongst 'Leavers' throughout the Referendum campaign which worked up immigration, increased diversity and British multiculture as being 'too much' and that immigration was having an impact on the everyday experiences of living and working for British people. There is now a growing body of research and literature (see for example Outhwaite's edited collection, 2017) which documents and examines the significance of immigration in relation to the 2016 EU referendum and the influence immigration had on the British public's decision to vote in favour of Brexit.

Secondly, the rejection of cosmopolitan elitism played a major role in the Brexit vote. There were many people who imagined that much of the problems and uncertainties happening within Britain were the fault of elite politicians. These people perceived politicians to be advocates of a 'global, corporate multiculture' (Neal, 2009) which favoured the expansion of globalisation and diversification over and above the protection of British interests and identity. Therefore, while this group of people perhaps did not vote in the

2015 UK General Election because they saw it as voting for much of the same, they voted for Brexit because it was not just a vote against the EU but also a vote against the Westminster government and reclaiming back localised expertise and maintaining security against the risks posed by globalisation as the British public know what is best for Britain and British interests.

This privileging of cultural sameness and rejection of elitism are part of Brexit's wider focus on the maintenance, protection and wanting of a particular type of British nationhood. The threatened Britain narrative evident throughout the 2016 EU Referendum not only represented a crisis of national identity but also displayed Britishness as a highly regulated, socially differential space that was valorised and sought after. Brexit reflects a specific type of Britishness that the British public extended some effort in constructing and controlling as to maintain a sense of security in an insecure world. However, despite the global changes that have happened in Britain and around the world since the last quarter of the twentieth century, there have always been strong associations between nationhood and differentially inflected social stability. And as I mentioned earlier, it is this which gets regularly and evocatively called upon in times of crisis and anxiety.

While calling on nationhood in light of global uncertainty appears to be a contemporarily 'new' phenomenon, it has been used historically as a way to secure the nation and assert national solidarity in times of crisis and anxiety. During World War One, for instance, it was a version of Britain and particularly southern Britain that was emphasised, mobilised and reasserted as 'home'. Howkins (1986) suggested that this idealisation of the south of Britain worked as an antithesis to the war-torn horrors happening in Flanders. The ways in which World War One worked with and produced an idealisation of British nationhood was multidimensional. It was threaded through wartime writing and poetry by the likes of Siegfried Sassoon, Edward Thomas, and Edmund Blunden, and was also there in the imaginings and dreamings of fields, lanes and cottages that soldiers would write about in their letters and correspondence home to loved ones. Likewise, in World War Two it was again the southern counties of Britain which provided the rich propaganda of the home/nation narrative that was being defended. You can see this by visiting museums like the Imperial War Museum of London which displays posters showing views of the South Downs with rivulets nestled against the curves of hills (see Neal, 2009). It is exactly these images that were selected to instil fortitude into the population and act as a visual reminder of British nationhood. The mobilisation of British nationhood in this way is not confined to extreme political moments such as war. As Murdoch and Pratt (1997: 56) state, 'the romanticism of nationhood is often portrayed as a civilised retreat [...] a zone where Sameness (British middle-class whiteness and heterosexuality) is reasserted in the wake of profound postcolonial anxiety'. It is possible to see this anxiety in the political reflections of the Populist Right in the lead up to and during the 2016 EU Referendum. Political figures such as the ex-leader of UKIP (United Kingdom Independence Party) Nigel Farage have commented on how being within the EU has brought with it specific threats to Britishness; threats which Nigel Farage denotes are brought about because of uncontrollable migration and the promoting of multiculturalism on part by the EU:

> We now have within many European countries, and dare I say, within the USA too, a fifth column living within our own countries, people, mercifully few in number, but people who are out to destroy a whole civilisation and our way of life…let's recognise the mistakes we've made. Uncontrollable migration, just not knowing in many cases who the people were coming into our country…the biggest mistake the government has made, we have promoted multiculturalism. We have promoted diversion in our society. We have said to large numbers of people, 'you can come here from any part of the world. Oh, by the way, please don't bother to learn our language; don't integrate in any way at all. You can take over whole parts of our towns and cities and we'll say it's made us a wonderful diverse nation.' That hasn't worked" he stated.

> (Taken from the Guardian, 2015)

These attempts by the Populist Right to mark out British national identity as perilously threatened can also been seen as a backlash towards the redefining and rebranding of Britishness through narratives of cosmopolitanism and multiculturalism which inflected the story of 'Cool Britannia' – packaged as a youthful, metropolitan, art, music and style renaissance – promoted by New Labour. More recently was the campaign for the 2012 Olympic Games in which London was presented and explicitly celebrated for its multiculturalism and diversification – it was 'the whole world within a city'. While these were both London stories rather than stories of British nationhood, it is the symbols of multiculturalism and diversity which the Populist Right have latched onto and denounced as representational of Britain and that ordinary Britons know what is best, not elitist politicians perceived to be pushing some sort of multiculturalist agenda.

This particular assemblage of British nationhood has held a long appeal for those on the extreme right in British politics. John Cato (1994, cited in Lowles, 2001: 150), for instance, a leading white supremacist who moved from London to a Lincolnshire village, writing in the irregular newsletter *Lebensraum* declared, 'home, gone from the scum and slime that is the nigger saturated London, its outreaches and Britain's other major towns and cities. We do not need to concern ourselves with Blacks, Jews, and communists. Or anything that they may fancy and do. Leave them to it. We are supposed to be Aryans, we should begin living as Aryans. As free spirits and men. Then we can reclaim our nation'. Likewise, the British National Party also tapped into this loss discourse around British nationhood, as is illustrated in the following extract taken from the British National Party's 2002 manifesto:

> You can't help but notice the presence of new housing development all over the country, destroying the character and in most cases the sense of community in the areas affected...But has anyone stopped to consider where all these people who are moving into these developments come from, who they are and why they are there?... [They are] people who see Britain as a refuge - a place to make a fresh start, away from the sordid, squalid towns and cities of their homelands.

What both of these quotations are doing is constructing a notion of Britishness as the last outpost of stability in a world which is becoming more and more insecure as processes of globalisation creep in and the need for it to be 'defended' as such. While the extreme right's interest in national identity and racist readings of it as a 'white spatial refuge' does remain relatively marginal, this idea of Britishness needing protecting from the tainting of multiculturalism and diversity fed heavily into the 'Leave' campaigns arguments for Brexit (see Chapter 1). In this case, it was the sanctification and associated regulation of British nationhood that was at the heart of the Brexit narrative about a country under threat which needed defending. However, this threatened Britain narrative that was the lynchpin of the 'Leave' campaigns platform does have wider implications on the exclusionary nature of British nationhood, and it is this which I now want to discuss.

Deliberations on the consequences of Brexit: Britishness as a site of exclusion

Under processes of globalised social change British nationhood has been decoupled from the conventional measures and markers of what Britishness is. The central theorisation has been on the ways in which Britishness has become unstable in light of global change but also how globalisation has aided the continuity of Britishness, people latching onto past ideals of what it means to be British to reaffirm a sense of security in a world that is perceived to be out of control. What I alluded to in the previous section is that the 2016

EU Referendum and the British public's decision to vote in favour of Brexit has exclusionary consequences. Brexit can be interpreted as creating British nationhood as a purified and sanctified space requiring (governmental) protection from perceived threats of globalisation.

It is arguments about geographies of purification and exclusion (see Sibley, 1997) which resonated throughout the 'Leave' campaigns with various contestations over the threatened Britain narrative. However, this 'threatened Britain' narrative from external globalised forces and political systems (e.g., the EU) has not always existed. In a post-World War Two environment, for instance, there was an optimistic and popular mood towards political change that demanded the joining up of Europe to militate any potential future conflict.

In the seventy-one years that have passed since the demand for the joining-up of Europe, we have had the creation of the European Economic Commission in 1951, which would later be subsumed into the birth of the European Union in 1993. While there has not been this envisioned United States of Europe, what did become of the current European Union has risen high on many great successes. The Cold War is over. The USSR has long been dissolved. A divided Germany has become one again. West and East Europe have been reunited. And freedom of movement and free trade became a lived reality.

Move forward to the present day, and some of the European Union's most prevailing achievements are now considered threatening to British nationhood. The most obvious example of this during the 2016 EU Referendum was the problematised presence of immigration. Migrants, specifically European migrants were worked up as an economic drain on key British institutions such as the NHS and that this justified the need for Brexit, and for Britain to be sovereign to balance and control the level of immigration and relieve pressure on British resources and institutions. This way of vindicating the relationship between Brexit, gaining British sovereignty and immigration contends with processes in which the protection of British nationhood worked in de-racialised ways. According to McCormick and Jones (1993), the term de-racialisation is used to refer to the duality by which 'race' is denied as a key referent in a discourse which is very much about 'race'. Within the discourse of the 'Leave' campaigns notions of 'race' are deemed irrelevant as Brexit and the resulting need to control migration was justified based on protecting and stabilising British institutions. The attempt by *Leave.EU* campaigners to extract or write out 'race' from Brexit revels the extent to which Britishness can deny and position itself as a (none) category outside of 'race' and ethnic thinking and identification. What writing out of 'race' from the Brexit narrative also did was actively shape a nation in which Britishness is valorised as an inert, culturally homogenous, 'forever Britain' place that is able to work as a symbolic space of identification that needs protecting from intruding globalised threats.

It is important to note, however, these exclusionary consequences of Brexit resulting from the protection of British national identity from immigration by claiming back sovereignty and control over its own borders is not a national story in isolation from the rest of the world. There are other, similar national narratives happening globally too – the election of Donald Trump in the USA in 2016, the political strides Front Nationale made in the lead up to and during the 2017 French Presidential Election and the growth of the Populist Right in countries such as Netherlands, Austria, and Poland. These movements, of course, have demonstrated the global scale of this threatened national identity narrative but, for the purpose of this book it is equally important to state that first, this threatened national identity narrative is more predominant in the British context and that this is because second, British nationhood is a colonial 'export' and 'comfort' that has been constructed and reproduced into specific colonialised landscapes of the UK.

So what are the material and everyday outcomes of this? The de-racialised discourse exhibited in the 'Leave' campaigns performs a number of concerning tasks: it denies and makes invisible the 'anti-immigrant' argument to the wider public who may have been inclined to be or be staunch supporters of Brexit; it severely limited the multicultural sensibility of the 'Leave' campaign through a discourse of protecting national identity and infrastructure as opposed to being out-and-out racists; and it sweeps under the carpet the longevity and proximity of Britain's colonial past. For example, stately homes and pubs were often built using acquired colonial wealth, and their interiors were influenced by and designed to reflect a 'colonial aesthetic' (Bressey, 2009). What the de-racialisation of the 'Leave' campaigns were most effective in doing, therefore, was producing a potent and reiterative narrative around the purification and sanctification of British nationhood that needed protecting from the globalised threats posed to them from the EU (e.g., immigration and limited sovereignty) and that a vote for Brexit was a vote for claiming back sovereignty and revalorising identity. While there may be of course constant challenges as well as quantitative and qualitative evidence that may disrupt and counter this particular narrative of Brexit, it is still this particular narrative which retains political and populist tenacity in the UK moving forwards into the Brexit negotiation process.

Conclusion

This chapter began by suggesting that the notion of British nationhood is constantly entwined with concepts of the social, the cultural and the ethnic. By beginning from this, I intended to give flavour to the argument which is at the heart of this chapter that British nationhood is constituted and structured by elements of social, cultural and ethnic identity and that it is these which are called upon in times of crisis and change to protect and secure Britishness. Bondi *et al.* (2005: 7) note that there is too close a connection between boundary forming processes of nationhood and social, cultural and ethnic markers of identity that it almost becomes productive to think that nationhood and ideas of social, cultural and ethnic identity are intrinsically related. This is because the very concept of nationhood is so invested with meanings and sense-making processes that it can work at a agential level between the actions, practices, and discourses of the individual and the exterior, structural reality constructed by collective populations; whilst also maintaining a primordial feel – that somehow nationhood is something which is both constructed and 'born and bred'. This is why 'home' works as a good metaphor for nationhood as it too works from the structuration perspective of a duality between individuals and wider social structure, that both nationhood and 'home' are constructed places of retreat and source for comfort and safety from ontological and existential risks and threats of which globalisation and social change throws up, but also both get mobilised in much the same way as a place of retreat, comfort, safety which constitute a feeling of primordialism; of recognisable and 'born and bred' belonging.

The multiple meanings of 'home' also reflect the ways in which nationhood can continually slip between and fold into concepts of social, cultural and ethnic identity and when combined they act as a way of ascribing those who can be marked out as culturally different, and nationhood gets used to mark out conditional sameness. It is important, therefore, to approach Britishness as I have attempted to demonstrate within this chapter as an assembled identity. Its very dominance means that defining the ways in which British nationhood is assembled is elusive because it is both multiple and mundanely located. As a dominant identity, it works most consistently and in its most delineated boundary in response to an idea of threat and so emerges most recognisably as a defensive narrative of an imagined past and endangered present (Gilroy 2005). This 'threat' is multiply located as well as ever present and creeps up at times when the boundaries around which Britishness are defined are at risk of being eroded. The most notable and recent example of this of which this chapter is based is Brexit. Within the narratives of Brexit, Britishness has tended to be deployed as being endangered from external threats of globalisation and European integration (e.g., uncontrollable migrations, existential risk of terrorism and reduced sovereignty), and essentialised as a symbol of what Britishness is or should be and this chapter has suggested that the vote to 'Leave' the EU was not just a vote in reclaiming sovereignty but also resisting wider processes of globalisation in order to maintain a sense of ontological security within an ever-increasing insecure world. However, the stories about globalisation, protection of identity and the resistance to change in recent events (e.g., Brexit) are not national narratives, they are happening locally as well within the English countryside. It is important, therefore, to start to map these issues around globalisation, protection of identity and resistance to change in the English countryside, and it is this which the next chapter will now go on to do.

Chapter 3

A Protean Countryside:
Community, rurality & social change

Introduction

Community is a troubled but durable social science concept. Part of its trouble – and its tenacity – is the concept's ability to connect with the ways in which people choose to make sense of theirs and others social relations and identity and how it stretches beyond the social world to academia which attempts to make sense of it. While community features across time and space (see, for example, Mooney and Neal, 2009), it also works as a potent container of, and symbol for, the ways in which rural social relations are organised. As Day (2006: 40) argues:

> places in which agricultural work is done, rural areas tend to be looked upon as long established, slow growing, close to nature, and in harmony with their environment, surely the most "organic" of human contexts… the rural type of social setting epitomises the social wholeness many expect from community.

What this chapter sets out to examine is that like the concept of British nationhood and Brexit, community works and becomes mobilised to protect rural identity from wider threats of social change. This chapter begins by acknowledging the assumptions, ambiguities and conceptual haze that are associated with the concept of the community before tracing the extent to which it has shaped understandings of the English countryside. From here the chapter explores how wider processes of social change that produce ontological insecurity and examines some of the potential threats this manifests for rural areas. The final section will argue that rural community, like nationhood, has an uncanny ability to work as a longing for 'traditional' forms of social relations; where, in a globalised world of upheaval, uncertainty and risk (see Cochrane and Talbot, 2008), the idealised image of rural community appears to offer security and stability.

Defining community

Any conversation about community should always start with a sociological disclaimer that it is a nebulous concept surrounded by debate. For example, Chavez (2005: 30) suggests that, sociologically, 'community has 'some 94 definitions', while Alleyne (2002: 608) maintains 'community is so fundamental a concept encompassing as it does myriad ways of thinking and talking about human collectivities that it is quite unsurprisingly a term which is impossible to define with any precision'. Accordingly, sociologists such as Stacey and Pahl (2006) have publicly declared their frustration with the concept and have urged a move away from it. However, this frustration has not led to a decline in social science's interest in community – this has continued to increase (see, for example, Crow and Allen, 1994; Bauman, 2001; Amit and Rapport, 2002; Day, 2006; Young, 2007). While it is not the intention of this chapter to map out in any extensive way the contestations over the community, it does commit itself to Alleyne's (2002: 608) important remark that 'community always needs to be explained rather than be the explanation'.

Community has held a constant place in sociological enquiry. It was a focus for Durkheim (1893 - reprinted in 2014), Simmel (1950) and particularly Tönnies (1953) whose association with the differences in social relations in rural and urban areas were outlined in his continuum of *Gemeinschaft-Gesellschaft*. For Tönnies, rurally organised, 'traditional' social relations could be defined through the concept of *Gemeinschaft*, which has been most commonly translated as community, and which was said to be defined through four core features – the biological, the geographical, the sociological and the psychological. In other words, these can be defined as blood, place, everyday interaction and sensibility (Bell and Newby, 1979; Neal, 2009). Each of these is familiar in terms of their continuing populist and political associations with contemporary understandings of community. Tönnies' (1963) critique of industrial capitalism saw the decline and loss of *Gemeinschaft* social relations as a key concern and a measure of society's shifts into modernity. 19th-century sociologists, however, such as Simmel (1950), 'viewed the city with more ambivalence seeing it as a site of "objective culture", calculation, rationality and blasé attitudes on the one hand but also as a site of cultural and social possibilities and freedoms on the other' (Neal and Walters, 2008: 283). Nevertheless, this *Gemeinschaft*-influenced concept of community – one tied to small-scale, mutual interaction and face to face reciprocal, interdependent social relations – has retained a particular folk and policy status. It has, as Bauman (2001: 1) elucidates, become a social relations ideal that works conceptually as 'the fireside by which we warm our hands'. Theoretically, though, the (empirically based) discontent that Stacey and Pahl (2006), and Bell and Newby (1979) articulated in relation to the concept has continued to drive processes of re-thinking how to interpret community as a descriptor of social relations effectively.

This academic unease with a *Gemeinschaft* version of community has meant that social science-led developments have seen community being moved towards the concept of boundaries (Barth, 1969); to a focus on its work as a symbolic cultural category (Cohen, 1985a); and to an analysis of its ability to represent largely imagined human connections (Anderson, 2006). The maintenance or otherwise of the boundary, symbols and imagined connections and the ways in which these give rise to insider/outsider dualities preoccupied much of the scholarly debate on the community during the 1990s and 2000s. Gupta and Ferguson (1997: 13) contend that 'community is...a categorical identity that is premised on various forms of exclusion and constructions of 'otherness', and accentuates that 'the strongest sense of community is, in fact, likely to come from those groups who find the premises of their collective existence threatened'.

Approaching community in such a way has tended to recast what community means – locating it much more in a 'beyond geography', non-*Gemeinschaft* context. Amit and Rapport (2002) maintain that this anthropological and sociological rethinking of communities has tended to shift the community studies discourse towards bigger themes of tension, conflict, exclusion or the mutations of identities and identity boundaries.

Nevertheless, what I am suggesting here is that although social science may be cautious about community and its ability, as a concept, to analyse social relationships this has not diminished its dominance within social science nor has it diminished its dominance in wider social and everyday settings. Neal and Mooney (2009) argue that community carries an intense attraction for politicians and policymakers, but it also has a 'folk' appeal. On this basis, it is crucial for social science to retain a concern with community and to be engaged by what it appears to be able to offer and gives it its populism. In other words, the community is impossible to ignore (even though the contentions as to how it gets used as an analytical tool for understanding contemporary social relations remains). It is with this in mind that the concept of 'rural community' becomes important to define. Rural community not only alludes to the small-scale, face-to-face social relations embodied in *Gemeinschaft* but also the way people make sense of it as a signifier for belonging and security which contemporary society is increasingly unwilling to provide (Bauman, 2001).

Theorising rural community

The most popular way to define rural community has been to separate 'the rural' and 'the urban' by depicting both of them as the two polarities of space. Rurality is commonly characterised by symbols of sociality, community, locality, familiarity, and close-knittedness, whereas urbanity is characterised by alienation and depersonalisation (Donnenneyer, 2007). Consequentially, this polarisation between rurality and urbanity have given rise to a rural-urban continuum, where some agencies such as the UK's Department for Environment, Food, and Rural Affairs (DEFRA) have attempted to demarcate the countryside from the city by using a six-point categorisation based on drive times and the size of settlements (see Table 3.1).

Cloke's (1977) index of 'rurality', based upon the analysis of multiple socio-economic indicators, provides insights into these characteristics and is considered symptomatic of the countryside. In Cloke's index, 'rurality' is defined by a 'series of distinct variables, including population, migration, land use and remoteness, which are measured to establish the extent to which an area is inclined towards the rural or urban pole' (Chakraborti, 2007: 5). However, while I agree that the concept of rural community does have a structural, place-based element; it is not without cultural sensibilities. For instance, Pahl (1966) asserts that such structural constructions of rural community arise from what he calls the 'village of the mind' (see also, Strathern, 1982: 250) – rather than an objective, measurable reality.

Table 3.1 – Summary of DEFRA's (2011) rural-urban classifications

Classifications	Definitions
Major Urban	Districts with either 100,000 people or 50 percent of the population in urban areas with a population of more than 750,000.
Large Urban	Districts with either 50,000 people or 50 percent of the population live in an urban area with a population between 250,000 and 750,000.
Other Urban	Districts with fewer than 37,000 people or less than 26 percent of the population live in large urban settlements and market towns.
Significant Rural	Districts with fewer than 37,000 people or less than 26 percent of the population in rural settlements and market towns.
Rural-50	Districts with at least 50 percent of the population live in remote rural settlements
Rural-80	Districts with at least 80 percent of the population live in remote rural settlements.

The concept of rural community in this case, therefore, can be understood as what Giddens (1984) calls a 'duality of structure'. Rural community is enacted in place (e.g., the countryside) which provides a structural context for individuals to emphasise the romanticism of rural life (e.g., rolling greens, hedgerows, and thatched cottages) that idealises the countryside as 'problem-free' (Chakraborti, 2007; Cloke, 1997; Scutt and Bonnett, 1996; Little and Austin, 1996; Cloke and Milbourne, 1992). These individualised idyllic connections, in turn, reinforce the structural representations that refer to the English countryside as an idyllicised space which provides shelter from the troubles of contemporary society. This is captured in the term the 'rural idyll', represented as 'happy, healthy and problem-free images of rural life safely nestling with both a close social community and a contiguous natural environment' (Cloke and Milbourne, 1992: 359).

Another way in which rural community has been 'romanticised' is through a direct comparison between city and countryside. As I have suggested, along with Chakraborti (2007: 10) in mind, 'dominant representations of rural community have tended to draw images of problem-free environments, but even when problems are acknowledged as existing within the rural sphere they are almost inevitably regarded as being external to the community' which seek to disrupt its stability. These external problems – e.g., diversity - are perceived by rural communities to be problems of more urban environments.

According to Giddens (1991: 43), fear is the response to these situationally specific threats which become connected with particular risks or dangers. Giddens argues that such perceived threats create uncertainty which arises from risk. According to Beck (1992: 21), risk can be defined as 'a systematic way of dealing with hazards and insecurities induced and introduced by modernization'. Hazards, according to Beck, are an unanticipated consequence of late-modernity, but unlike hazards of modernity which were bounded to certain localities or limited to specific groups, late-modern hazards span across time and space. Therefore, whereas processes of diversification were once restricted to urban areas, the development of late modern society has meant that these processes of change can reach more ruralised contexts which brings with them suspicion and fear of the 'urban'.

This distrust of urbanity has been a constant theme in the rural studies literature. Murdoch and Marsden (1994), for instance, describe urban spaces as uncertain and unstable where people are unlikely to achieve any real sense of security. Murdoch and Marsden (1994) go on to maintain that this may be the reason why people have desires to seek alternative forms of space. Antithetically, rural community is portrayed as a safe haven from the problems associated with urban living, a place which emphasises 'a timeless, stable and enduring sanctuary from the city, detached from contemporary culture and firmly anchored in a mystical, if not mythical, vision of the past' (Scutt and Bonnett, 1996: 2).

This 'vision' of a rural community, as noted above, is evident within radio and televised media, where the idyllic and quintessential representations of rural community have long been exaggerated. Chakraborti (2007), for example, highlighted how Bunce (1994: 50-55) depicted the nostalgic character surrounding televised and radio programs such as *The Archers* and *All Creatures Great and Small* which emphasise the 'quieter side' of rural living and kinship, and the way Fish (2000: 17) used the work of Jones (1997) to explore the enduring appeal of the countryside in the television adaptation of *The Darling Buds of May*.

What such televised and radio media is doing is disseminating the idealisation of rural community life to the wider British public; and in addition, by producing and reproducing the idyllic constructions of the countryside as antithetical to the urban experience (Fish, 2000: 19). Consequently, these romanticised and idealised understandings of the rural community are perceived to be threatened by the wider processes of social change in a contemporary, globalised world.

Social and spatial change in rural areas

Kingsnorth (2005: 12) in the report *Your Countryside, Your Choice* denoted the scale and scope of globalisation happening in the English countryside by witnessing 'the remorseless expansion of housing, industry, traffic, road building and airport construction, combined with the steady decline of traditional farming'. However, these processes of globalisation within the English countryside are nothing new. Priestley (1939: 165) commented on the concern of globalisation facing rural England at the end of the 1930s in his essay *Britain is in danger* where he described how the urbanisation of the twentieth century had spoiled the English countryside.

Compare this with Askwith's (2007: 6-7) account in his book *The Lost Village* where he recalls the lines from Philip Larkin's poem *Going, Going* and thus his feelings of loss, on coming back to the Northamptonshire village in which he resides. In this Askwith observes how he had always assumed that his rural village with its own unique social relations and landscapes and memories and its own peculiar way of saying and doing things would always be there. But, through people's embrace of the late-modern world, he is saddened to realise that the place where he lives a sense of rurality had all but gone.

Similarly, Kingnorth's (2011), *Real England,* expresses what he sees to be the indictment of the countryside by the encroachment of global, corporate market forces. Kingsnorth (2011: 154), like Askwith (2007), argues that there has been an erosion of rural life in which while the mental image of rural England still composes of 'hay meadows, gambolling lambs, poppy fields, spinneys' and 'a curious, almost childlike country landscape: part Beatrix Potter, part Rupert Bear', we can still feel 'its heartbreaking power' as individuals do not know or want to know how eroded English rurality actually is.

What Askwith (2007) and Kingsnorth (2011) are reflecting on in their books, however, is an idealisation of rural community life. They are romanticising the niceties of rural life without paying heed to the harsh realities of rural living: cruelties of nature, rural poverty, extreme weather, and social isolation. They are both merely tapping into common preconceptions in people's narratives that are somewhat based on the myth of rural life and belie the often-harsh realities of rural living. Nevertheless, it is these common preconceptions of rural life that provide security and comfort against the social and spatial change happening in rural areas and the perceived loss of rural community. These anxieties about social and spatial change and the impact of globalisation on the English countryside do not only imbue a sense of loss about rural community, but they produce a sense of fear. These fears arise from perceived social and physical threats which mitigate the types of behaviours and attitudes typical of rural community life. Below I want to spend a little time mapping out some of the wider threats to rural identity.

A 'plurality of rurality'

One of the primary factors of social change that has caused feelings of loss of rural identity is what Chakraborti (2007: 17) calls, the emergence of a 'plurality of rurality'. Along with the expansion of geopolitical borders (the European Union), car use and cheap air travel there has been an increase in the transnational movement of people. Consequentially, as globalisation ties time-space (Giddens, 1984) together with people, unrecognised to 'traditional' rural spaces, can freely come and go as they please; meaning, there is greater plurality in the voices and lived realities being expressed and heard in the countryside (De Lima, 2008).

Many studies (see, for example, Magne, 2003; Neal and Agyeman, 2006b; and Chakraborti and Garland, 2004) have touched upon the pluralising of rural populations. Magne's (2003: 31) study in Devon, in particular, highlighted that minority ethnic individuals living in rural areas had increased by 100 percent during the 10 years from the 1991 census to that of 2001: an increase that demonstrates the changing, and evermore diversifying demographic of the English countryside. Similarly, Neal and Agyeman (2006b) observe, using data published by the Countryside Agency's 2004 *State of the Countryside* report, that there was a '14 percent growth in the ethnic and racial rural population between 1981 and 2002 compared to a corresponding 3 percent increase in urban areas'.

In the context of the pluralisation of rurality, the most important impact on population growth in rural communities has been the influx of Eastern European migrants following the expansion of the European Union in 2005. This is supported by Vargara-Silva and Markaki (2015) who assert that the number of Eastern Europeans in agricultural employment in rural areas, such as Norfolk and Suffolk, is approximately 1.9 million.

Neoliberal expansionism

The rise of service based industry and the expansion of neoliberalism is also perceived to be threatening rural identity. While there is no universal definition for neoliberalism, many academics (see, for example, Hasenfeld and Garrow, 2012; Midgley, 2001; Mullaly, 2007; Ritzer, 2000) agree that it represents support for free-market capitalism and privatisation. Commentators such as Kingsnorth (2005) have expressed concern that such levels of expansion in rural areas will make the 'traditional countryside all but disappeared by 2035'. These types of concerns about service-industry and the erosion and loss of rural identity can also be read in Scruton's (2000: 254-255) account of contemporary rural life, where he denotes how the rural imagery of England's past (e.g., the hedgerows, thatched cottages, the family farm, the firefly, the nightingale, the barn owl, the eagle, the roadside reptiles and hedgehogs, the newts of the ponds and skylarks of the meadows) has all but disappeared and that rural England has become 'a no man's land, an 'elsewhere', managed by executives who visit the outposts only fleetingly, staying in multinational hotels'.

Therefore in rural areas where Gemeinschaft social relations are most likely to be played out, the effects of neoliberalism which put business interest first and foremost are likely to have the greatest impact. This is because neoliberalism does not care about the social relationships of local rural communities; it sees the countryside as an opportunity for making money regardless of whom or what is affected. Such processes are reflected in news coverage and current soap storylines. For example, in 2014 an episode of *The Archers* radio show picks up on much of these fears of neoliberalism facing rural areas. There was a story around the incursion of big business into the rural landscape with a new by-pass cutting through the village which was likely to attract other commercial businesses threatening both the spatial (dividing David and Ruth Archer's farm and jeopardising its viability as a milk producing enterprise) and them selling up and moving out breaking the long-standing social connection of the Archers family with the village.

Housing and rural planning policy

With the membership base of rural areas increasing and the spread of big business, there has been greater demand for housing in the countryside. Consequently, local residents have started to organise and mobilise tactically (Lowe *et al.*, 1993: 117), by using local controls to protect and maintain their 'idyll' from encroaching development of housing that is perceived to be eroding the natural beauty of local rural character. Such action is often labelled 'NIMBYism' where residents display what is popularly known as Not in My Backyard attitudes (Derounian 1993).

The reason for such action is that the countryside can be seen as what Hirsch (1977: 9) termed a 'positional good': a space in limited supply where its consumption is contingent on people's attachment to it (Hirsch 1977). Hirsch provided a similar analysis of the suburban dilemma, where an increase in the occupation of suburban homes would be a detriment for all the others. Ultimately, the more popular an environment becomes, the less desirable it's setting. Thus, the appeal of the countryside can only continue if its access is restricted to all other groups.

The emphasis of marketisation, therefore, by the Thatcher government in the 1980s, which allowed local councils to relax green belt policies to accommodate the development of housing (Elson, 1986), paradoxically preserved the countryside through green belt policy which had made it neoliberally attractive to businesses and individuals in the first place. For instance, in Blunden and Curry's (1988: 85) study, they concluded that such marketisation led to:

> a limited number of linked, medium-sized growth areas set in a sea of general rural restraint... it is just this policy of protecting the character of the countryside which has made the area so environmentally attractive to both indigenous and incoming high-tech firms.

We can see these types of resistance to processes of (perceived) deterioration; or at least fear of it, happening in many rural towns across the United Kingdom. For example, in 2013 the Independent reported that plans to build more houses in a green belt area which lay across three villages – Gaydon, Lighthorne and Lighthorne Heath – in Stratford-upon-Avon: 'urban life is threatening to invade their country retreat, in the form of a plan by Stratford-on-Avon District Council to fill those 44 acres with a "green village" including 4,800 homes'. Consequently, the residents of these three villages were in an uproar over the loss of their local identity, with one resident commenting:

We fully appreciate that houses have to be built somewhere, but we were told that the policy was to be a fair distribution, not to distribute them in a way that would devastate any one community. If this development was in London, it would stretch from the Houses of Parliament to St Paul's Cathedral. There will be at least 10,000 cars going through the village to the M40.

Another notable example of this apparent NIMBYism is in Hubbard's (2006) study in rural Nottinghamshire and Oxfordshire where opposition to the proposed local development of asylum centres sparked anger and rejection of them because they felt they were, as Cloke (2004: 34) puts it, 'out of place in the countryside' and could be more appropriately built in an urban context. Thus the opposition towards the building of asylum centres in Hubbard's study served to reaffirm a rural area regarded as unsullied, safe and 'problem-free' which reinforced the romanticism of the countryside.

Culture of individualism

The influence of urbanisation and neoliberal expansion on rural communities has created a culture of individualism (Halsey 1995; Kingdom 1992; Saunders 1990). As the contemporary world turns its focus onto the individual and corresponding decline of the state as responsible for the delivery of social wellbeing – the result of Thatcherism in the 1980s – it has been accompanied by a heightened sense of 'absence of society' (Bauman, 2000). As the role of the welfare state diminishes in the United Kingdom within a discourse of individual enablement, opportunity and responsibility a general mood of risk and the unpredictability of the world has increased (Cochrane and Talbot, 2008). On our own, managing the concerns of social and economic status – un/employment, wellbeing/illness, the educational attainment of our children, old age, the fluctuations of global markets, falling and rising house prices and so forth – all add to a sense of an insecure world stalked by risk and threat.

Jock Young (2007: 12), commenting on the disjuncture between affluent western societies and the rise in senses of insecurity within them, has described it as a kind of social vertigo – 'vertigo is the malaise of late-modernity: a sense of insecurity of insubstantiality, and of uncertainty, a whiff of chaos and a fear of falling.' Young (2007: 12) argues that living this disjuncture has resulted in a more fearful and reactionary social mood. This reactionary social mood has developed because social relations are no longer restricted to the locale and can instead be re-articulated across wide time-space distances (Giddens, 1991). Car use and cheap air travel have had a detrimental impact on social interaction in rural areas (Neal, 2009). It has made possible the 'mixing' of cultures, which in turn has facilitated the growth of rural settlements and increased difference, thus reinforcing social fragmentation and social separation (Neal, 2009). Urbanisation and neoliberalism exacerbate the separation of the individual from the wider rural community; and, as a result, some rural areas become less – although imaginably - synonymous with being socially caring communities, but rather more indicative of distrust, aggression, and misanthropy (Neal, 2009). This engenders exclusion and exclusiveness (Halsey, 1995), as evidenced in the work of Tyler (2006) and Hetherington (2006).

Social media, the internet and the notion of virtual rural communities in a digital age

The growth of technological communication has further increased feelings that we are living in a culture of individualism. The development of the internet has radically changed the dynamics of social life (James, 2014). Central to the critical role of the internet is its access to information resources. Never in the history of humankind has there been an opportunity to access virtual libraries on a plethora of subjects and partake in 'virtual communities' from which we can connect with anyone, anywhere in the world. This, along with continuous improvements in technology, ensures that information resources and social networking opportunities through the internet are 'exponentially increasing' (Edwards and Bruce, 2002: 180). For instance, there are more than 5 billion Google searches and more than 500 million tweets and Facebook posts per day (James, 2014).

This digitalisation of social life has had a huge impact on rural areas (Rice, 2014). Traditionally rural areas have been defined as cohesive communities based on close-knit social relations and bounded by shared physical space (Skerratt and Steiner, 2013; Johansen and Chandler, 2015). However, as the use of the internet has increased, more and more people are using technologies and social media websites such as Facebook and Twitter. The use of these websites has been accompanied by and contributed to, significant shifts in rural social relations. For example, today, people living in even the most remote rural areas can exchange messages from their computers, tablets, and phones to other individuals living on the other side of the world (James, 2014).

This compression of time-space created by the internet has facilitated a fear of the diminution of the rural community. There is a perception that the digitalisation of rural life has weakened social ties (Cumming and Johan, 2010), and created further atomisation between individuals living in rural areas. Woods (2007) suggests this is because the internet deteriorates social bonds through only providing 'bite-sized' interactions, such as posting tweets which are only 250 characters in length, which do not allow for social bonds to foster and develop. Moreover, the growth of online connectivity has the ability to blur the boundaries between insiders and outsiders in rural spaces. Anyone can join a rural community group on Facebook and Twitter from anywhere around the world, increasing concerns regarding the arrival of newcomers in rural areas within which long-term residents have little understanding whether an individual or group of individuals are local or not (Dargan and Shucksmith, 2008; Shucksmith, 2010; Johansen and Chandler, 2015).

While the rise of the internet and social media has changed the dynamics of rural community life, it has also facilitated its continuity. Social media platforms such as Facebook and Twitter have rearticulated the ways in which rural communities construct their identity. Such a process involves the public posting of (and response to) various experiences and understanding of, interests and investments in and questions and concerns about rural community identity and social relations. Take, for example, a picture of a rural landscape. As a picture, it does not necessarily foster a sense of rural community and identity but does more so when posted onto a social media platform, such as Facebook, for individuals to collectively reminiscence and construct an identity onto it through the posting of comments. In this respect, practices of constructing rural identity online are the product of what van Dijck (2013: 402) calls 'the culture of connectivity...where perspectives, expressions, experiences and productions are increasingly mediated by social media'. And as van Dijck has stressed, as part of a wider networked techno-culture rural community does not disappear but rather carries on through patterns of interaction that are co-constitutionally enmeshed in technological systems commonly designed to inscribe particular social and cultural interests.

Given the increasingly pervasive character of this culture of connectivity, it has become commonplace for people to use social media to construct virtual versions of 'real life' rural communities. Like 'real world' rural communities, the construction of online rural communities has social implications, such as the production of exclusive and exclusionary boundaries (Sibley, 1997). Despite the perception that the advent of virtual rural communities has blurred the boundaries of insiders and outsiders, they have actually continued to perpetuate it. For instance, when creating community groups on social media platforms such as Facebook, community membership can be either open or closed therefore allowing those with a greater vested interest in the community to deny access to individuals unrecognised by other community members actively.

Life and character from social change

Historically, the rural community studies literature (see, for example, Arensberg and Kimball, 1940; Rees, 1950) has been largely silent on the impact of these threats of globalisation on life and character of rural communities. Arensberg and Kimball, and Rees presented the themes of family, kinship and neighbourliness as core to explaining local social systems in rural settlements and both argued that these were cohesive, interdependent and complete or whole social systems. It is this completeness that gives the inhabitants of Llanfihangel yng Ngwynfa – the parish that formed the basis of Rees' study – their sense of belonging and social bonds. Rees' (1950: 168) study, in particular, was the first to denote a sense of weakening social ties and imminent change under the influences of a globalised society.

Although Bell and Newby (1979: 140) suggest that Rees (1950) overstates his anti-urban position in addition to straying too close into 'community as normative prescription [rather] than empirical description' they go on to argue that Rees 'can be considered the founding father of the British rural community study – over the next fifteen years the prefaces of most studies acknowledge a debt to him'. Rees' account of Llanfihangel can be read as a contribution to a 'golden age' metanarrative of the rural community story. For example, Rees (1950: 91) emphasises the mutuality between neighbours and the home as key to the community in Llanfihangel in which friendliness and helping neighbours played a central role in facilitating a rural community based on modes of sociality and conviviality.

Rees' (1950) study has value too in terms of its observational descriptions of aspects of social relations in remote rural locations in the 1930s and 1940s. Rees stresses the importance of conviviality and hospitality – the community is based around informal sociality and organised in homes: 'home has been the place at which people gathered for a noson lawen (merry evening), for religious devotions and above all for conversation' (Rees 1950: 100). Rees' Llanfihangel research was influential in later studies of rural populations and should be recognised as marking a recasting of the anthropological gaze away from the exotic other of colonial contexts and onto the familiar social geographies of 'home'.

However, the tendency that Rees (1950) exemplified towards the telling an observational story of an anti-urban cohesive rural community was further developed in the research of Williams' (1956) study of the rural community of Gosforth in the Lake District. According to Williams, Gosforth could be understood as a 'close-knit', face-to-face based rural community. But, as Bell and Newby (1979: 202) point out, for Williams, as for Rees (1950), there is a worry that the stability of Gosforth is likely to shift and change as urban and outside influences negatively have an impact on these localities with 'a loss of community feeling because of these developments'.

While Bell and Newby (1979) are critical of the absence of quantitative measures by which to compare these early community studies, what is more striking well over half a century on is the extent to which the notion of imminent change to rural populations – particularly from an urban outside – casts a perennial shadow over these studies. Unlike Rees (1950) and Williams' (1956) studies which do not engage with the processes of social change within local rural communities but which rather assert the interactional wholeness of those communities, later studies engaged more fully with the ways in which globalised social change created processes of stratification defined by notions of division, boundaries, and outsiders. Newby's (1979) study of farm labourers in East Anglia was one of the first that marked the beginning of this repositioning of both the method and theoretical focus. In arguing that a class analysis based on land and property ownership was as relevant in rural societies as urban ones Newby argued that the English peasantry had, since the 19th century, been replaced with a class system and social division between the working class agricultural labourers and the distinctly middle-class of farmers, landowners, and professionals (clergy/teachers/incomers). While for Newby this meant that conflict had to be viewed as integral to rural social relations, he argued that this conflict was to greater and lesser extents contained by the dominance of the authoritarian and deferential narratives of the rural community. Newby (1979: 46) argued that community could be seen in the ways in which working-class agricultural labourers had 'a strong sense of shared occupational experience, a distinctive occupational culture, an overlap between work and non-work roles and loyalties, and a prevalence of closely knit cliques of friends, workmates, neighbours and relatives' which enabled attachment to place to form that were largely a function of geographical and economic necessity as a result of living in rural isolation and poverty, thus promoting values of mutual aid and neighbourliness.

Alongside this version of a local rural community of fate and necessity, Newby (1979) suggested it was possible to see another narrative of the rural community in which both labourer and landowner/farmer could all belong. This narrative is one which focuses on the whole village and its territorial geography which folds social inequality into this. Likewise, Strathern (1982) focused on notions of kinship and belonging rather than a class in her Elmdon study, but like Newby (1979), she too found a series of social stratifications. For example, Strathern identifies four broad (and class corresponding) social groupings in Elmdon – 'real Elmonders' (born and bred in Elmdon families); 'Elmdoners' ('real Elmdoners' which had married in outsider family members before 1914); working-class newcomers (post-1914) and middle-class commuters and retirees (post-1914). However, Strathern argues that these boundary mechanisms between the social categories of Elmdon society interacted with, rather than were defined by, land and property ownership. From this Strathern (1982: 253) argues that Newby's (1979) narrative of 'whole rural community' imposed from above by the property classes was not seen in Elmdon as 'real Elmonders' resisted this and spoke of a divided village while middle-class incomers did claim that a village community existed. Yet Strathern (1982: 253) does concur with Newby in her acknowledgement that there are specific cultural elements to the construction of rural belonging that are largely shared amongst all resident groups. In other words, there was a broad agreement about what it means to be a "villager" or "outsider," and most of the inhabitants subscribe to the idea that the village is bounded.

The emphasis on rural community as being a category for conceptual rather than concrete meaning of identity and the emphasis on rural community's ability to exclude - especially those who are outside of its boundaries – as a result of globalisation and social change are themes that resonate throughout this book (see Chapters 5, 6 and 7). One other example of this within rural community research has been Bell's (1994) study of the Hampshire village of Childerley in which he reveals the stark class-based social stratifications within Childerley. He describes it as a 'slightly feudal village' in which it was possible to trace a clear divide of affluent, overwhelmingly middle-class 'haves' and poorer, overwhelmingly working class 'have nots'. Bell (1994: 58) describes the village as having 'a two-class system: 42 percent 'have nots' and 'ordinary people' and 58 percent 'haves' and 'moneyed people'. Bell saw these divisions reproduced in a myriad of mundane, social practices some of which were reflected and reinforced in the use of the local pubs – the quieter and upmarket Horse and Hound pub - and the noisier and much more basic – the Fox Inn - which working-class residents used.

These class divisions were apparent to Bell (1994) in other everyday habits and lifestyle behaviours. For example, Bell discusses how village residents and their families and friends using either the back door or the front door to gain entry to their houses can offer a number of cultural and class readings. Similarly, the way in which gardens are designed and tended and used by their owners and the ways in which landscape and 'the view' was or was not explicitly appreciated offer insights into the social stratifications within Childerley. For example, Bell (1994: 172) observes that 'there is something about the spirit of land as the landscape that feels more right to the moneyed villagers [...] In other words seeing land as the landscape is a bit of power trip...something that feels right to the socially powerful'. These material and class divisions and the social conflicts – most often expressed through tensions felt by working-class residents as to village activities being organised and/or taken over by middle-class residents – that stemmed from these were ones that were openly acknowledged by all the residents that Bell spent time with.

But what is more striking is that the residents of Childerley felt uncomfortable and ambivalent about the issues of class identity and class-based practices. It was the source, then, not of certainty but great unease – as Bell (1994: 86) puts it: 'while all the village residents recognise themselves as members of social classes, in general, they do not feel good about it'. However, this moral ambiguity about the social stratifications in Childerley was partially resolved for the residents – middle and working class alike – by recourse to a discourse of being more than anything, a 'country person'. Its polar opposite was being defined as a 'city person'. To belong to the category of 'country person' was a way of being bound into a broader belonging to Childerley itself.

Bell (1994: 92) suggests that the category of 'country person' is important as it required a dual commitment to a notion of local community and a close affinity and attachment. This translated into a proposition that in peaceful green settings social relations are small scale, face-to-face and thereby richer and more caring and able to transcend social divisions – 'there is helpfulness in country life most villagers agreed, a unity that ties residents together across class lines'.

The enduring appeal of rural community

In a roundabout way, these powerful and emotive feelings of threat (Milbourne, 1997) tend to provoke people to emphasise the idyllic characteristics of rural living (Sibley, 1997; Murdoch and Pratt, 1997). This can be seen in the way former prime minister, John Major, cited George Orwell's portrayal of British rural life as 'county grounds, warm beer, green suburbs...and old maids cycling to Holy Communion through the morning mist' (Garland and Rowe, 2001: 121).

References to idealised and romantic notions of 'invincible green suburbs', 'warm beer' and maids cycling through morning mist can be interpreted as alluding to the idea that as worries about the potential threats and the irretrievable loss of rural identity grow so too does the appeal of a rural community (Bauman, 2001). These worries are themselves part of a broader contemporary social insecurity. They are worries about the loss of particular types of idealised communities. This is captured in Rees' (1950: 170) final comments on the social changes that Llanfihangel faced. In an unequivocal indictment of urbanism, he argued that the urbanity had failed to provide residents with status and significance within a functional society. Thus, the English countryside – with its offer of a more complete social order involving the cohesion of family, kindred and neighbours – was able to promise the individual a sense of belonging which the diversification and uncertainty of urbanised social worlds could not readily provide.

This fantasy of place, social ties, and belonging is a potent one then and has become ever more potent as the rural communities of contemporary society appear as very different to those organic, rural ones of the past. Of course, as we have seen from the discussions of Elmdon and Childerley, rural communities are not quite the complete social world Rees would present. Nevertheless, as the potential threats to rural identity intensify so does the importance of a notion of rural community that depicts a desirable way of life. Clarke (2009) suggests that the yearning for the rural community can be understood through four popular desires: restoration, security, sociality, and solidarity. Each of these is co-constitutional and convergent, and each reflects and is inflected by a series of contemporary anxieties and troubles. For example, in using the term *restoration* Clarke (2009) argues that people's idealisation of rural community taps into notions of the past, a time of more orderly social relations defined by 'proper' social conduct and social authority. But not only were social relations perceived to be more mutual and warm they were also appropriately deferential, and this produced wider stability. This notion of a loss of a better way to be and behave relates to and reinforces the idea that community delivers senses of security. It is important to reiterate, of course, that, much like Kingsnorth (2011), Clarke (2009) is referring to people's idealised preconceptions of rural community life without giving attention to the extremities of rural living, such as rural poverty and cruelties of nature.

In this context, as the rural community has come to matter more – it becomes a form of social retreat as well as a site of sociality. Clarke (2009: 35) argues that this sociality is not necessarily about the nostalgia of the golden age *per se*, but is more about a wanting of better, and more transparent, social relations that go beyond the 'alienated, calculating and mediated' forms of being together that appear to characterise twenty-first century social bonds. Certainly, this notion of shared social bonds has been one that has been applied to rural communities as we saw in the findings of Newby (1979) and agriculture workers in East Anglia. However, as discussed above, these social bonds can be mobilised around a whole range of social issues and concerns to protect identity. Thus, in the contemporary social world, a traditional rural community is ever more sought after, but something contemporary society is not willing to provide (Bauman, 2001). Even in the warm glow of *Llanfihangel*, Rees (1950) was already troubled by the shadows and shifts of the processes of globalisation.

Furthermore, people actively in search of the community tend to be committed to its visibility and to making it visible and expend effort and imagination into this task. For instance, in Lanfihangel the sociality that Rees (1950) describes was of the hearth and home, between neighbours and kin, and even this was giving way to more self-consciously constructed social bonds. In contemporary rural contexts visible community tends to be actualised by the self-conscious community-creating efforts of 'busy' individuals, social organisations, local events, the church and so forth (see Chapter 5 for an examination of community-making and identity reaffirming efforts around a local rural carnival event). Both Strathern (1982) and Bell (1994) observed community-making labours in Elmdon and Childerley and both noted the irony that the efforts to create community through mainly middle-class driven activities of organising the village fete, the harvest festival, the tidying up of the village graveyard and so on, actually led to new divisions and resentments and senses of local customs and concerns being taken over by those moving into the village from outside. But in many ways, it is these efforts to make a community that are important. That people do yearn for and expend considerable effort in the actualising rural community does need to be attended to and acknowledged. We can note its silencing of internal dissent and difference, and we can note its inevitable boundary construction and its highly problematic constant excluding and including dynamic, but for me, it is the appeal of community that remains crucial to keeping in mind when talking about inclusion/exclusion. We cannot simply dismiss the search for and construction of community as parochial, inward-looking, reactionary and defensive practices – although these may indeed each or all be part of community-making processes too – as Jock Young (2007: 128) puts it 'the building of community, its invention, becomes that of a narrative which celebrates and embraces one side and vilifies and excludes on the other'.

In the above quotation, Young (2007) is comparing past communities with contemporary ones. He notes that the former were face-to-face, intergenerational, embedded in the locality and local identity and expressed informal processes of social control; whilst, in contrast, the features of the latter are difference, fragmentation, pluralism, and transience. Young, here, is speaking of community in urban settings. But what happens if we apply this to rural settings? Would it be so different? It would be possible to suggest that communities both of the past and today in rural settings were more convergent of the features identified in Young's two lists. Wealth and poverty were very much features of rural settlement. Transient and mobile populations have also been much more part of rural environments than popularly assumed. Not only because of some of the social changes of enclosure and clearance and changes in agricultural production but because agriculture itself has always required labour on an intermittent and seasonal basis – agriculture has a tradition of using low paid migrant labour which it maintains today. The rural communities of the past were more mobile, divided, heterogeneous and chaotic than they are now recalled as being.

Likewise, the fragmented, pluralist, mediated, contemporary rural communities are not completely without a social dimension or face-to-face interaction or a local identity or senses of belonging being expressed by those that live in those areas. The current policy and political interest in social capital reflects some of this aspect of social relations in rural settings. For example, in Moseley and Pahl's (2007: 23) study, they identified ways in which contemporary 'social patterns and process in small rural places help to produce distinctive bases for social identities and social cohesion' in which they found - to greater and lesser extents – 'organic' community dimensions in all four of their rural case study areas. For example in one Shropshire rural town - Bishops Castle – Mosley and Pahl argue that there was a significant bond that had arisen between 'ordinary people' keen to organise the local festivities of the area. In a direct echo of Rees' (1950) Llanfihangel findings, Moseley and Pahl (2007: 23) also emphasised the importance of the informal: 'The key feature [of successful social capital] is informality based on trust; people seem to come together and get on with tasks with little or no formal organisation in the accepted sense'. My point here is a simple one. While the perceptions and experiences of risk and uncertainty and precariousness within the English countryside have produced heightened senses of ontological insecurity, these have driven desires for a rural community to model its romantic past. And it is this what people latch onto in order to protect who they are or who they want to be.

Conclusion

The central thrust of this chapter has been to suggest that, like the concept of British nationhood and the use of Brexit to maintain ontological security and reconstitute a sense of British identity in a globalised world, at a time when rural community is becoming increasingly atomised under processes of globalisation (Neal, 2009; Kingsnorth, 2005; 2011; Woods, 2007) which has led to a perceived loss of community and social fragmentation, people look to rural community to construct an identity. I started this chapter by defining the concept of community. I addressed the issue of community as both place-based (spatial) and imagery (social) and went on to discuss the impact social change has had on the concept of rural community. I noted that processes of social change - population growth, neoliberal expansion, the internet, planning policy, and individualism - have all imbued a sense of threat within the English countryside. I also expressed how this all gives rise to fears and anxieties about loss of rural identity and the consequences of life from social change; whilst, at the same time indicated how people latch onto this idea of rural community as a way to keep a hold of the past.

The focus on everyday processes of producing and reproducing rural community has been an effort on my part to demonstrate the link between British nationhood and Brexit, and how rural communities act/respond to issues of globalised social change and how they maintain ontological security. Indeed, like British nationhood, we are able to see the notion of the assertion of rurality as a defensive concept running through the positions articulated by Neal (2009) and others. This connection between the way rural and national identities are defended, marked out and valorised in light of wider social changes happening globally inflects a need to perform a 180 degree turn back towards a contextualisation of the ways in which identities are maintained and protected despite being perilously threatened by globalised social change. It is this that Chapter 4 now considers by drawing references to the ways informal social control is enacted in a context of maintaining and protecting identity from wider processes of globalisation and its exclusionary and racist consequences.

Chapter 4

Controlling Identities:
Informal social control, exclusion
and racism

Introduction

This chapter builds upon the discussions of Chapters 2 and 3 that drew parallels between British nationhood and rural community in relation to issues around social change by theoretically mapping how communities and nations enact informal social control to resist globalised social change and protect identity. The influence of the Chicago School of Sociology on the study of informal social control and deviance is significant. However, there is a need to rethink some of its theoretical and methodological approaches as this gives space not just to explore them elsewhere, but also to incorporate aspects of environmental criminological theory to explain informal social control outside the domain of crime management.

This chapter is organised into two sections. The first considers what informal social control means. It does this by firstly examining the historical context of informal social control by exploring its theoretical and methodological use within the Chicago School and environmental criminology, which maps the spatial distribution of crime and disadvantage and sees communities as sites of informal social control that either enables or militates crime. Such a historical context is important as it acts as my point of critique. That is, to understand the particular significance of informal social control in relation to identity management it needs to be reconceptualised in a 'beyond crime management' way. What the first section of this chapter aims to demonstrate is that much of the theoretical and methodological applications of informal social control can be applied elsewhere, to the study of rural communities and nations, change and social identities. This section does this by drawing on the sociological concepts around spaces of governance, governmentality, and territorialism that see communities as sites of boundary-making, of external threats and internal dangers by which informal social control is enacted to protect against the diminution of the community from wider processes of change. The second section goes onto examine the exclusionary consequences of informal social control. Within this section, a contextualisation of exclusion is made before positioning racism as one of the potential social harms that derive from it. From here the literature around structural and institutionalised forms of racism is covered to demonstrate that the exclusionary consequences of informal social control and the racisms that they give rise to are not rooted in racist victimisation or racial othering, but rather a result of resisting change and protecting identity.

The Chicago school and environmental criminology

The Chicago School of Sociology was the first to see the empirical importance of informal social control to the study of community relations. Shaw and McKay's (1942) application of mapping techniques led to the development of social disorganisation theory based on their observations that rates of crime in the inner city remained constant despite high rates of population turnover. Social disorganisation theory viewed crime as a normal response to the breakdown of social relations and the diminution of community caused by urbanisation and population growth. Foster (1995: 564) suggests that informal social control is 'a powerful inhibitor to the commission of crime' and the inability of communities to effectively communicate traditional norms and reproduce informal social control meant that criminal values could flourish through transmission to new generations of residents (see Klinger, 1997; Wilson and Kelling, 1982 also). Similarly, differential social organisation theory focused on community as key sites of informal social control, and Shaw and McKay argued that criminal values were communicated to young people through close proximity to those who engaged in or sanctioned criminal behaviour, an unavoidable consequence of living in the inner city.

Taking this further, Shaw and McKay (1942) maintain that the restraining influence of family was undermined by the presence of alternative value systems presenting deviant means of success and rendered impotent by the close association of boys with delinquent friendship groups which could command greater loyalty. This enabled the coexistence of conventional and criminal worlds due to the dependency of some families on the illicit incomes of some members, which further reduced their efficacy as a site of conventional social control (Browning *et al.*, 2004).

The Chicago school identified population turnover as a key factor behind the breakdown of informal social control. Zorbaugh (1929) detailed such consequences of frequent population turnover and changing social dynamics around Chicago's lakeside. In this, he illustrated that while the wealthy Gold Coast residents demonstrated mechanisms of informal social control despite low population turnover and community members residing elsewhere during the summer and winter months, in the slums where a plethora of different people and cultures passed through, the churches were the only institutions where some mechanic of informal social control was evident. Other organisations that existed, such as clubs and gangs, were representative of segmental as opposed to communal interests and so did not act to bring people together. Zorbaugh argues that because of this lack of self-governance, more formal means of control (e.g., the police) were used to protect against greater deviancy and criminality.

The literature on environmental criminology elaborates further on these Chicago school theoretical concepts. Bottoms *et al.'s* (1976) ethnographic research within Sheffield in the UK, for instance, clearly describes the importance of friend and kinship networks for the transmission of criminal values through generations and to newcomers on some of Sheffield's more notorious and deprived council estates. One important finding of this study is the demonstration that two estates, nearly identical in terms of population and socio-economic factors, had very different crime rates, suggesting that poor areas can indeed reproduce informal social control despite the popular view of these places as being uniformly disorganised, high crime areas. Bottoms *et al.'s* research found that several factors lie behind the differential crime rates between the two council estates in Sheffield, with specific importance given to the allocation mechanisms between and within the public-private tenure types. Those estates with the best reputations built up longer waiting lists, with the result that most of their new tenants were those who wished to improve their situation by moving to a more sanitised area from their present council estate. This helped foster prosocial norms and perpetuate the desirable image of estates such as 'Stonewall', whose origins as an artisan area privileged it over the slum appearance of estates such as 'Gardenia' despite their shared status as social housing estates. This led to 'Stonewall' becoming considered a stable, low crime rate area.

In contrast, those tenants with the highest social need and thus least able to avoid unpopular areas, such as young families, often found themselves in either high-rise blocks (e.g., the 'Skyhigh') or local, criminally notorious estates (e.g., the 'Blackacre'). The transitory nature of the former was found to instruct anomie, and the latter's stable criminal culture was reinforced through the transmission of criminogenic values to new residents, which was in turn maintained through the housing allocation mechanism. Many Blackacre residents were long-term and had strong family ties, thus propagating the criminal subculture. Elsewhere, the chance allocation of a couple of 'problem families' into a previously well-regarded area precipitated a downward spiral as those tenants who could leave did so and the pool of potential incomers became increasingly restricted due to the area's worsening reputation.

Bottoms *et al.'s* (1976) analysis of the mechanisms of housing allocation is crucial to understanding how many of the key elements of the Chicago school's theorising on informal social control were relevant to the British context. Social disorganisation theory finds its vindication in 'Gardenia', where the repeated socialisation of the estate's children in school and on the street meant that criminal values were transmitted to newcomers and further perpetuated the bad reputation of the area. The transitory nature of the high-rise tower blocks also created a socially unstable environment where norms could not flourish, and which was criminogenic for the younger residents.

Bottoms *et al.* (1976) uncovered the presence of criminal networks and a level of tolerance for these activities as long as they did not involve the victimisation of neighbours. However, Foster (1995) notes that this may have been due to a fatalistic attitude on the part of some residents regarding their own ability to enact control or to move away. Foster's study in the deprived Riverside estate also demonstrates how local control capacities are in part dependent on the supportive actions of authorities with the capacity for formal sanction against more serious transgressors; in Riverside, the local housing authority took action against problem neighbours. Atkinson and Flint's (2003) study in a pair of affluent and deprived estates in the cities of Glasgow and Edinburgh back up this link between formal and informal social control, which rather contradicts popular perceptions of antagonistic relations between the police and poorer communities that harbour oppositional norms. Instead, Atkinson and Flint maintain that the presence of a law-abiding element was identified within those deprived areas which sought to enact informal social control against predatory elements or who wished for formal sanctions to be applied.

Furthermore, Hope and Foster (1992) examined the changing levels of crime on a deprived housing estate as part of the *Priority Estates Project* after changes were made to the built environment, the quality of management and to the social mix on the estate in the project. They found that despite contributing to a decline in population turnover, there was also an increase in evidence of crime and disorder (Hope and Foster, 1992: 495). For instance, physical improvements such as cosmetic improvements and the creation of defensible spaces increased levels of control; whilst at the same time, a local influx of young tenants brought together the adult and youth subcultures on the estate and consequentially intensified levels of crime.

Moving beyond crime management

While informal social control has been previously conceptualised in criminology as a crucial part of crime management in communities, it has a much wider context than that of crime. It also encompasses actions used to protect and reinforce identity. Simmel's (1950) concept of *Sociation* refers to the informal ordering of everyday life, the moral codes and conventions, and the interpersonal relationships and ties that bind people together. He argues that the individual is at once within society and yet against it, as society acts as a force which curbs his or her autonomy it also acts to aid their individuality. This is perhaps best summarised by Simmel (1950: 10) as 'a process which continuously emerges and ceases and emerges again', meaning that it is the myriad small, everyday interactions which tie individuals, and therefore communities, together. A community is simply the result of these many interactions which become permanent and begin to assert their own laws, and Simmel (1950: 13) claims that 'all these phenomena emerge in interactions among men... they cannot be derived from the individual considered in isolation'.

In considering informal social control from this perspective, Simmel (1950: 9) argues that the variation between individual and group behaviour is not just factually different, but also has normative and moral significance. He differentiates between morality, wider structures, and customs, where morality develops inside the individual who confronts him or herself as a knowing subject; these normative forms then attain autonomy, or become 'customs'. The contents of these behaviours are then valuable because they are what ought to be, and so they become 'objective' (e.g., the structure of community). Morality is simply one form of the intrinsic and extrinsic relations of the individual to his or her social group (Simmel, 1950: 100), and in different contexts, the content of this relation become law or custom. Simmel uses a continuum, with opposite poles of law and morality, and in between stands custom, from which both are suggested to develop. 'A group secures the suitable behaviour of its members through custom, when legal coercion is not permissible and individual morality not reliable' (Simmel, 1950: 101) and belongs to smaller groups, where breaching this custom is of concern to others, as opposed to subject to legal sanction by all of society. Custom relies on public opinion and individual reaction and so can only be executed by small groups.

Black (1976) and Cohen's (1985b) understanding of informal social control broadly correspond to Simmel's (1950) definition, with Black (1976: 2) arguing that informal social control represents 'the normative aspect of social life, or the definition of deviant behaviour and the response to it, such as prohibitions, accusations, punishment and compensation' and Cohen (1985b: 3), while advocating against a broad definition of informal social control that encompasses all the ways in which power is enforced amongst individuals in society, extends the work of Simmel (1950): 'organized responses to delinquency and allied forms of deviant and/or socially problematic behaviour which are actually conceived of as such, whether in the reactive sense or in

the proactive sense'. The focus of Cohen's work is that images and vocabularies of the community are co-opted by society as a means through which to
define as well as control deviant groups (Cohen 1985b).

Moreover, Becker (1963: 60) argues that the majority of informal social control is not coercive, but instead acts by shaping the perceptions and attitudes
people have of the soon-to-be-controlled activity and the feasibility of engaging in it and is communicated by those whom the potential deviant respects.
This approach highlights the primacy of the social group as a key actor of
informal social control and is in sympathy with the work of Braithwaite (1989)
who argues that shaming mechanisms are both culturally specific and work
best within community settings as long-term residents tend to have invested
more personal capital in these relationships, and so the shaming or informal
social control of actions resonate more strongly.

Chriss (2007: 44) argues that communities are the primary vehicle by which
informal social control is enacted, and his definition of informal social control
draws on this: 'all those mechanisms and pressures of ordinary, everyday life
whereby group pressures to conform are brought to bear against the individual'. Implicit in all of this is a move away from environmental criminology's
definitions of informal social control, and instead identifies informal social
control as part of social relations that tend to gravitate towards the produc-
tion/reproduction of a collective identity which acts as a key source of control
from perceived social problems, such as the erosion of identity from globalised change.

Spaces of governance, governmentality and territorialism

Sociological theories around spaces of governance, governmentality, and
territorialism are useful in understanding rural communities and nations as
sites of informal social control. Governmentality refers to the responsibilisation of individuals into conformity and the obligation of adhering to existing
structures within a community. Through this process of responsibilisation,
residents/citizens are empowered to act in a moral capacity as guardians of
the community by looking out for each other and to enact shared oversight
within the community. Consequently, communities/nations become spaces
of governance in which norms and social structures are both internalised and
externalised by those residents/citizens who have a shared psychological and
emotional investment in the place.

Despite attempts to integrate theories of spaces of governance, governmentality, and territorialism into the wider 'threatened identities' literature (Edwards and Hughes, 2005), this remains a minority perspective. However, these
concepts are important in helping conceptualise the exclusionary consequences of informal social control. Stenson (2005) notes, for instance, the

importance of local networks in the fostering of informal social control, particularly kinship and peer networks in the context of declining state responsibility (such as the promotion of Theresa May's 'Shared Society' rhetoric) as breakdowns in the interdependence of state and civic society result in community or other social networks that provide alternative forms of governance (Lea and Stenson, 2007).

The governmentality literature (e.g., Rose, 1999; Innes, 2003; Stenson and Edwards, 2004; Hughes, 2007) discusses community as a site of informal social control in terms of how individuals can be encouraged to internalise norms through appeals to their communal allegiances, either from local social institutions or the community itself. David Garland's (1996) concept of 'responsibilisation' can be understood, in this respect, as government efforts to encourage communities and individuals to take on local problems without state interference. For instance, 'Shared Society' suggests that it is no longer the responsibility of the state to help with community matters, but rather the collective responsibility of every individual. However, one impact of 'Shared Society' on increasing the self-regulatory capacities of communities is that it is often those individuals with greatest emotional and psychological investment that take on-board self-regulation as a mechanism to protect against unwarranted social change as to reaffirm the norms and identity of their area or country. It is at this individualised level that the reproduction of informal social control has the potential to be most effective, and indeed exclusionary.

Foucault (1977: 22) discusses the internalisation of norms and the development of techniques of discipline designed to create 'docile bodies'. He argued that by controlling space, it is possible to foster self-control into individuals in which it will alter the way they conduct themselves in the future. The internalisation of norms is also a feature of governance literature. Crawford's (2003) concept of 'contractual governance', for instance, elucidates that conformity with rules and social order can be enacted through routines and daily practices. He argues that contractual governance attempts to construct compliance by embedding individuals into a web of parochial social contracts through which they pass during their daily lives. Consequentially, a sense of moral responsibility towards one's own community defined in terms of emotional ties and cultural allegiances manifests.

Power operates through this construction of compliance with community norms. Anthony Giddens (1984: 293) defines power as 'the means for getting things done and, as such, is directly implied in human action'; thus, pertaining to an individual or group's 'ability to structure the behaviour of themselves, and to be able to resist the structuring capabilities of others' (Farrell and Bowling, 1999: 256). Thus, power, especially in the case of Brexit, refers to the mechanisms being used (compliance) by those with greatest vested interests to construct British nationhood; whilst subverting the actions and behaviours of individuals of those who choose to be controlled. Informal social control, therefore, draws on the capacities of the community to achieve a consensus on a normative order and then acts to reproduce, maintain and protect it, and does so in a wider context of socio-spatial change, as is the case in Brexit. Such production and reproduction of normative social orders within community spaces are manifested through both individual and structural approaches, and it is these approaches which the next section goes on to detail.

Community, structural, ideological and cultural controls

There have been two key criminological works which have examined the influence of informal social control on the protection of identity (see Burchfield, 2009; Steventon, 2001). These studies have suggested that informal social control, defined, as the willingness by residents/citizens to intervene in problems concerning the country or local areas is an important factor in protecting particular social identities. Steventon (2001) maintains that structural, ideological and cultural controls were important in the protection of identity in the suburban context of his research. Using the definition put forward by Shapland and Vagg (1988), Steventon (2001: 209) identifies structural, ideological, and cultural controls as 'the processes that maintain conformity or compliance with the norms, values, and standards of the culture or community'. Steventon expressed in his study that conformity or compliance with the norms of the suburb was rooted in the early socialisation of inhabitants and the development of social bonds. Using a case example of two teenage women he elucidated how these social bonds had an influence on the way they conformed to the expectations of their peers (Steventon, 2001: 211-212).

Burchfield (2009) found similar structural, ideological and cultural processes of informal social control in her research within an inner city, urban area. Her research highlighted that it was not early socialisation or the development of social bonds that enabled informal social control, but rather an attachment to the local area. Burchfield suggested that the attachment inhabitants expressed towards the neighbourhood highlighted the distinctiveness of the area and the feelings about the neighbourhood that residents felt. In this, Burchfield (2009) found that attitudinal attachment in the form of perceptions of the neighbourhood as a place to live, and sentimental attachment are important features of informal social control to protect identity. Attitudinal attachment, in particular, was stated as having a positive effect on levels of informal social control. Burchfield argued that deep levels of attachment to an area might have a mediating effect on experiences of social change, perhaps on the basis of erosion of local identity, which increases attachment and the willingness to reinforce informal social control in defence of such identity.

Alternatively, community controls can be understood as the individual properties of communities (Giddens, 1984) which produce, reproduce, and are enabled by structural norms, values, and customs. Burchfield (2009) did not discuss community controls, but in Steventon's (2001) study these were the actions local residents used to protect their suburban identity. Steventon commented on how local residents came together to resist change in a planning application which would see housing designs shift from detached houses to terraced houses that threatened to sell at a price that would allow lower socio-economic people into the suburb. Steventon highlighted that desires to protect the suburb's identity (community controls) were produced and reproduced by the attachment residents had to the suburb (structural, ideological and cultural controls) which, in turn, made the resident want to protect the identity of the area (community controls).

Active and passive controls

Steventon (2001) highlights that structural, ideological, cultural and community controls can be both either active or passive. Again, using Shapland and Vagg's (1988: 66) definition, Steventon (2001: 191) defines active informal social control as controls which include a range of activities involving ''watching', 'noticing and defining', 'making decisions as to action', and 'taking action'', whilst identifying passive informal social controls as the dominant norms of the community. In other words, passive informal social controls are 'all the processes people use to shape their particular culture or ways of doing' (Shapland and Vagg 1988: 66).

Steventon's (2001) understanding of passive modes of control relate to what Giddens (1984: 290) calls 'practical consciousness'; or what people know about their own action but are unable to articulate. Thus, passive informal social control accounts for the practical actions people do without the need to justify and rationalise such actions. Such actions, therefore, refer to the structural, ideological and cultural controls discussed above. Conversely, Steventon's (2001) notion of active informal social controls reflects what Giddens (1984: 290) calls 'discursive consciousness'; or the extent of what people know about their own actions. While Burchfield (2009) did not mention the influence of such active processes of control, Steventon's (2001) analysis of them was apparent. These active processes of control tended to about people's discursive attempt to militate crime in the suburb (Steventon's (2001: 207-208). However, Steventon (2001) clearly evidences that the active processes of control are not so clear-cut. He found that most often actions to militate crime led to unintended exclusionary consequences of protecting identity. And so it is a contextualisation of exclusion which the chapter now turns to.

Contextualising exclusion

The primary consequence of informal social control is that they give rise to an exclusionary and sectarian dynamic whereby communities become divided in terms of insiders and outsiders. In order to understand the exclusionary consequences of informal social control, however, we must first define what exclusion means. According to Taket (2009: 28), 'in order to understand the dynamics of exclusion and connections across different layers of human action, it is important to reflect on how these concentric spheres influence each other and the common pathways which run through them'. In other words, to define exclusion one must first conceptualise the connectedness between people. One way individuals draw connections between each other is through the production of social capital. Putnam's (2000: 34) model of social capital sees the connections people have as 'social glue' and 'social oil'. 'Social glue' is understood by Putnam as cohesive practices that are shared by individuals with social similarities, including similar values and ideals and similar activities and mutual relationships. On the other hand, 'social oil' is defined as the networks, cooperation, and reliance between different people/groups.

Likewise, Bourdieu (1986) describes social capital as first, relationships that enable access to resources, and second the production and reproduction of such resources. Social capital, therefore, is contingent on investment in order to produce structures of social capital that cumulatively create outcomes of social action and connections. Social capital is thus a result of both the continuity of interactions within a community context and whether or not such interactions pervade the sphere of specific groups and/or particular individuals.

Furthermore, Halpern's (2009) model is complementary to both Putnam's (2000) and Bourdieu's (1986) framework of social capital as it combines components, functions, and levels. Components are the networks, norms, and sanctions of communities. Functions draw on Putnam's (2000: 34) notion of social capital as 'social glue' and 'social oil' in order to understand how power relationships are formed. And levels cover the interaction between the microsocial – familial ties, neighbours, and friends – and the macrosocial – community; or, to put it another way, the top-down processes, structures and sanctions that influence individuals but which are produced and reproduced by them.

This co-joined relationship of social capital is useful for identifying and understanding the complexities of what constitutes exclusion as it emphasises the embeddedness of capital and cohesion processes. Social capital is not a straightforward process and can be both inclusive and exclusive; affinity with and membership of particular groups or communities or nations can reinforce inequalities, enforce power without a mandate and produce norms, including the ability to exclude as well as include. Putnam's (2002: 34) notion of 'social glue' in particular may exacerbate exclusion by protecting the boundaries of the dominant social group and identity of a particular community. This definition of exclusion gives rise to what Foucault (1980: 215) termed 'technologies of power', where the interaction between individuals and structure become forms of control. Social exclusion is thus a result of the outcome of norms, values, and morals that are institutionalised and routinised over time and space through ingrained traditions and customs. The person's likeliness to be included or excluded from community life, therefore, is contingent on their identification/lack of identification with or ability/lack of ability to achieve such values.

Defining racism

Racism can be understood as one of the potential social harms of exclusion. Commentators such as Allport (1979) define racism as the feelings and images of difference that inform a set of prejudicial ideas and beliefs about certain groups of people. He affirms that prejudices emerge from generalised anxieties of difference that have happened all through history. Allport (1979: 7) contends that the foundations of prejudices are regularly situated inside the defensive cognitive processes of the individual, and can be defined as '…an aversive or hostile attitude towards a person who belongs to a group, simply because he belongs to that group, and is therefore presumed to have the objectionable qualities ascribed to the group.'

What Allport (1979) is referring to here is that despite the fact that the fanciful apprehension of certain groups of people is a good and beneficial human quality, it is equally a damaging one where imagined fears cause genuine suffering to others. Allport (1979: xvii) suggests that there is no answer for the state of human prejudices in which 'it is simpler, somebody has said, to crush an atom than a prejudice'; therefore, illustrating the naturalistic predisposition of the human mind to bring order and security to an insecure 'runaway' world (Giddens, 2002; see Chapter 2 also). He contends that this produces a mental overload in which the human mind attempts to categorise objects as either good or bad.

However, such a naturalistic approach to viewing racism has been criticised. Klein (1986:182), for instance, asserts racism does not occur in nature, but rather it is learned, constructed, produced and reproduced. In advocating Object Relations Theory, Klein maintains that human minds are capable of splitting objects into good and bad, from which produces an idealisation of the good and a sense of fearfulness of the bad. Both Wetherell (2003: 105) and Sibley (1997: 5) advocate a similar perspective in which they argue the social and material world is developed through psychological perceptions of 'otherness' and 'sameness' and that this leads to internalisation of specific social and spatial boundaries.

The notion of fear of difference as learned behaviour was a fundamental finding of New Labour's Community Cohesion Agenda (Home Office, 2005) which explored the antecedents to the Oldham race riots in 2001. Commentators like Cantle (2005: 8) acknowledged that little was achieved to address the issues of racism. In fact, exclusion was the cause of people retreating into 'comfort zones' (Ouseley, 2001), which consequentially enabled racism to occur as the result of a diminution of trust, mutuality, and conviviality.

Dozier (2002: 41), using the lens of social identity theory, sees racism as an inevitable process in a contemporary globalised world where he explains how wider societal pressures and strains cause individuals to separate into 'in groups' and 'out groups'. Allport (1979), conversely, sees this as ultimately leading to the naturalisation of discrimination against the 'out-group'. These psychological explanations of racism, nonetheless, are based on visible minority ethnic individuals being problematic; whereas the racist discourses surrounding the exclusionary consequences of informal social control to maintain and protect identity from wider processes of social change are more structurally and institutionally ingrained forms of racism.

Structural and institutional forms of racism

Structural and institutionalised racisms are – by and large - the production and reproduction of historical and contemporary societal beliefs that possess the ability to become racist through the way they are embedded, enacted and institutionalised within everyday life. Despite the majority of evidence about institutionalised racism predating Macpherson's (1999) definition, *The Macpherson Report* was important in recognising the social and historical context around which particular institutions, such as the criminal justice system, have, albeit unwittingly, allowed the perpetuation of domination and control. The MacPherson Report found that racism is rooted in the legal profession (King and May 1985), concluding that there is a clear tradition of institutionalised racism embedded within key governmental agencies within the United Kingdom. This is concurred by Kundnani (2007: 5), who suggests ideas of control are entrenched into the socio-cultural fabric of major social institutions which systematically adhere superordination to the 'in-group' and subordination of the 'out-group. Academics, such as Bowling (1998: 29) assert this has ultimately transformed 'the legacy of colonialism into indigenous racism'.

These institutionalised forms of racism are problematic enough when set in an institutional context, but as Plastow (2011) argues they are then further exacerbated in rural and national contexts because rurality and nationhood are typically constructed as landscapes of hegemony where minority ethnic individuals do not belong. Accordingly, when both social and spatial boundaries within rural England or Britain respectively, under the current contemporary rhetoric of 'global, corporate multiculture' (Neal, 2009: 230), become threatened, it is the actions used by long-term residents and citizens to protect and maintain their associated identities which enact unintended, institutionalised forms of racism.

Conclusion

What this chapter has attempted to provide is a contextualisation of the ways identities (both rural and national) can be maintained and protected against wider globalised change through the enactment of informal social control and their exclusionary and racist consequences. This chapter did this through re-examining informal social control. While the focus of the Chicago school of Sociology and the literature on environmental criminology has been on how communities enact informal social control to deal with and manage crime; there is scope to view informal social control through a 'beyond crime management' lens. I argued that the key dynamic, in this context, was on how some long-term rural residents (and indeed British citizens) react and respond to globalised change and uncertainty and where the maintenance and protection of identity within a specific context can be achieved through modes of informal social control.

Furthermore, this chapter has also highlighted the exclusionary and racist consequences of informal social control. This second section provided a contextualisation of exclusion in which I drew on the wider sociological literature around the social capital to provide rich and valuable insight into the nuances of exclusion and racism that operate out of informal social control. The discourses of the wider sociological literature have highlighted how racism can occur as the potential social harm of exclusion. From here, the chapter succinctly mapped out the definition of racism as a process of fear of difference and how this stretches beyond the fear of difference to the way racism is structured and institutionalised into the discursive and practical actions of individuals, communities, and nations.

Thus far in this book, I have denoted the relationship between Brexit and rurality (see Chapters 2 & 3). I have argued that Brexit was not just a national story. Brexit was the result of wider social changes happening across Britain, in different and multiple localities and the ways in which residents of these places responded to and attempted to resist such changes. Chapter 3, in particular, articulated the ways in which notions of community and rurality have been used and mobilised in similar ways as nationhood in times of globalisation and uncertainty, and this chapter has conceptually mapped how (rural) communities and nations successfully enact modes of informal social control to maintain and protect their identity from its perceived erosion by social change. For the remainder of this book, then, I want to draw on empirical evidence taken from the rural community of Brickington to demonstrate how all of this theorising about rurality, community, social change, informal social control, exclusion and racism has parallels with the way Britishness and Brexit have been used to construct a narrative of an 'identity under threat' and the ways this narrative has been mobilised to resist globalised social change perceived as threatening to the ontological security of the place.

Chapter 5

A Night at the Carnival:
Maintaining local rural identity in the face
of social change

Introduction

In Chapter 3 I described the threats of social and spatial change on rural identity; threats which are widely portrayed in the sociological, criminological and
geographical literature as increasingly precarious to the erosion of the 'traditional' English countryside (Kingsnorth, 2005; 2011; Neal, 2009; Askwith,
2007). The central thrust here was to demonstrate the tangential but nevertheless connected discourses between loss and/or threats to rural identity
and people's ability to romanticise the countryside to emphasise the enduring appeal of rural identity. For example, current debates that appear to be
about contemporary ontological insecurities in English rural society such as
individualism, senses of precariousness (Bauman, 2000; Young, 2007); the
urbanisation of rural areas, the technological revolution, and the impact of
global corporate culture (Davis, 2005; Clarke, 2009; Cochrane and Talbot,
2008) can, as Chapter 3 set out to demonstrate, all be seen to be present in the
contemporary longing for rural England.

In order to understand the processes surrounding how informal social control was enacted to resist globalisation and its exclusionary and racist consequences, I know I needed to study a rural town undergoing a major change.
Brickington was a small, but developing rural town in the south of England.
Brickington's primary composition was made up of seven settlements. The
historic town centre, Albury, and the 19th-century expansion make up the
centre, while the Commons, Bay, the Vale and the Marsh are positioned on the
town's peripheral. All of which is bounded by wide open green space (split
between a number of paddocks and fields) which made Brickington aestheti-
cally rural in character (see Figure 5.1).

Such composition, however, did not always exist but rather grew from continual development. The ribbon development in the 1930s and the immediate
years following the Second World War served as the swansong to Brickington's
rural character. Further development in the 1940s and 1950s saw the town

sprawl awkwardly outwards, and much of the newer houses and buildings being built were insensitive in design to local character. For instance, newer housing estates were built using national standards of design and often made from a random mix of materials (e.g., white concrete and reconstructed stone) rather than Brickington's more 'traditional' character (e.g., red brick and coarse rubble houses).

Figure 5.1 – Brickington: housing boundaries

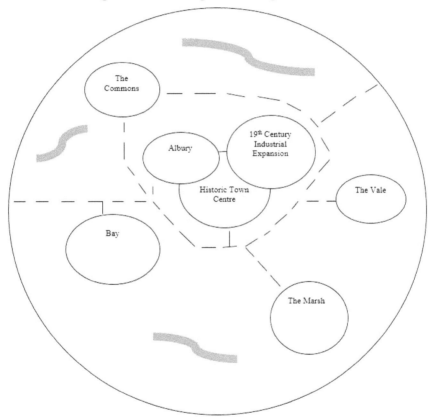

Key:

Open, green space (fields and paddocks)

Author's own

The rationale for choosing Brickington, therefore, pertained to the on-going developments and changes that were happening within the town. According to the local archives, Brickington was once furnished with a variety of shops – a butcher, a shoemaker, a greengrocer and other daily, local rural amenities – which have steadily declined since 1945, many of which disappeared during the 1960s.

In the late 1970s new industry – such as a life science and human technology company and a lighting factory – came to the town. Land was released for housing developments and the town started to grow. The 'Relief Road' provided the opportunity for a supermarket, and other service-based industry to be built on the fields situated along the road. In the 1980s, a Waitrose store opened and soon attained the position of the third busiest Waitrose in the country, and became a focal point for future development (see Figure 5.2).

The expansion of Brickington continued into the 1990s and 2000s and has seen an increase in housing developments in the town, with another 1500 homes built in 2016 to meet the migration of populations from wider geographical areas such as London and Poland. There is a need to be careful not to overstate that migration patterns from outside Brickington were the root cause of housing development in the area. Developments would have been constructed to house local residents due to the gradual growth of the population over time (Gkartzios and Scott 2013). Nevertheless, Brickington had witnessed a growth in population from 9,940 in 2001 to 11,756 in 2011. This growth of population is not isolated to Brickington and can be seen in surrounding towns. For instance, Hillsbury's (five miles away from Brickington) population has risen from 5,219 to 7,707 and Newton's population from 2,433 to 4,355 (see Table 5.1). However, what makes Brickington exceptional is that much of the town's growth has come from an influx of individuals from outside of the area, with the majority of growth coming from minority ethnic groups (representing 6 percent of the total population of the town) compared to 4.5 percent of the total population of the county (see Table 5.2).

Most of these groups have been brought in on the back of local social change and tend to occupy the housing estates on the peripheral of the town, while those who are a longer term or born and bred in Brickington live in the centre. This can be seen in my final sample of participants which comprised of twenty-six residents ranging in age from late-teens to early-eighties and varied self-perceived ethnicity and social status types including: six minority ethnic individuals, three wealthy retirees, ten people who had moved from London, and seven born and bred residents (see Table A.1).

Figure 5.2 – Brickington: physical infrastructure

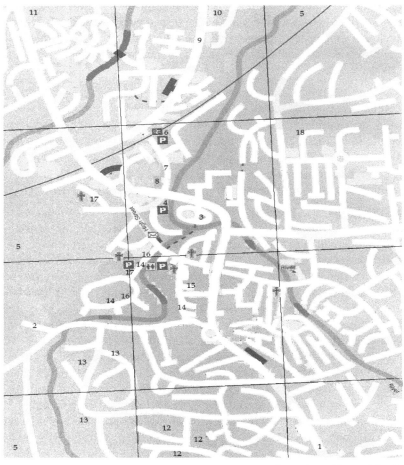

Key

1. The Relief Road
2. Bay Lane
3. Waitrose
4. Asda
5. Fields & Farmland
6. Railway
7. Station Road
8. Italian cafe
9. New Road Business Park
10. Garden centre
11. Attached houses (Fields Estate, Cherry Tree Lane)
12. Bungalows (Shreen Way & Sylvan Way)
13. Victorian terrace houses (Kings Street, Barnaby Road, Weavers Avenue)
14. Cottages (Cottage Lane)
15. Suburban Villas (Barnaby Road, Weavers Way)
16. Detached cottages (Barnaby Road, Thomas Hardy Lane)
17. Semi-attached houses (Orchard Lane)
18. Semi-attached houses (Orchard Lane)

Author's own

Table 5.1 – Brickington population compared to surrounding areas

Settlement	Total population (2001 census)	Total population (2011 census)
Brickington	9,340	11,756
Hillsbury	5,219	7,707
Newbury	2,433	4,355

Taken from County Council's (2011) website

Table 5.2 – Ethnic diversity of Brickington population compared to wider county

Ethnicity	Brickington	Wider county
% of white-British	94.0	95.5
% of Black and Minority Ethnic (BME) groups	6.0	4.5

Taken from County Council's (2011) website

In this first chapter of three chapters which examines how informal social control is enacted in the English countryside to resist social change and maintain a sense of security and rural identity, I maintain that in Brickington threats of social and spatial change endangered a particular local identity whilst concurrently allowing for its maintenance and enduring appeal. I begin this chapter by contextualising what 'Brickington identity' is. The importance of 'Brickington red brick' buildings and natural elements of the locality will be discussed to make sense of how some residents work up Brickington's rural character and how such meaning is imposed and constructed. An examination of some residents' perception towards social and spatial change (e.g., housing, service industry, and competing interests) will be explored, and this will be followed by a case study of the local carnival. The case study will offer insight into the ways Brickington identity is symbolically bounded into the carnival to capture what the town should represent to provide ontological security in a time of uncertainty in the local area.

What is Brickington identity?

Amit and Rapport (2002: 60) have argued that 'community identity is conceptualised first and foremost by reference to what is held in common by its
members rather than in terms of oppositional categories between insiders
and outsiders. What matters most is what 'we' share, not the boundary dividing 'us' from 'them' (Amit and Rapport, 2002: 60). There is some of this shared
experience going on in the construction of Brickington identity; drawn from
the collective ways some residents' associations of stereotypical features of
rural life (e.g., fields, red brick building, and thatched cottages) were used to
fix the town with a rural rather than urban identity.

Such shared experience of community created symbolic boundaries. These
symbolic boundaries of Brickington identity were produced by the 'ongoing
togetherness of beings and things' (Jones and Cloke, 2001: 651); in other
words, the way some residents spoke about the local character of the Historic
Town Centre and surrounding area, and the effective and emotional feelings
the area had on them. The local character of the Historic Town Centre was
characterised by late-Victorian architecture; constructed from the coarse
squared rubble with clay tiled roofs and Ashlar dressings (see Figure 5.3 –
picture on top). According to local archives, the availability of Brickington
brick from the local factories in the second half of the 19th Century meant
that the main walling material changed from rubble to brick. Initially due to
its high cost, it appeared only as dressings to windows and doors; however, as
production increased and prices reduced, it became the main material. Em-
bellishments were incorporated consisting of stone lintels, mullions, and
quoins, detailed brick or contrasting coloured brick. Generally, roofs have
been clad with plain clay tiles, with some exceptions using slate or, in only a
few sites, thatch. Windows were also generally timber sash (see Figure 5.3 –
picture on bottom).

Many of the residents interviewed identified the importance of this 'red
brick' character, and it is this what some residents focused on when describing Brickington identity. For example, Barbara highlighted 'In the middle of
the town you have these traditional red brick buildings, and this is what
makes Brickington for me'. Likewise, Irvin very articulately described the 'red
brick' nature of the Historic Centre as 'a gem':

> If you look at the centre of the town where Kings Street is, there
> you have traditional red brick buildings and thatched cottages
> as well as a beautiful stone church. And this continues all the
> way past the High Street. That area of the town is very tradition-
> al and is quintessentially Brickington.

Figure 5.3 – Local Character of Brickington

Photos taken from Brickington Neighbourhood Plan (2012)

Deborah also discussed the connections she felt when exploring and looking at the local 'red brick' landscape:

> Looking at the buildings that were once here and reading about
> the red brick that was manufactured in the town, and the old
> quarry tiles, that sort of thing. That's what made Brickington
> unique.

Similarly, Julie expressed an attachment to the architecture of the historical
town centre:

> I love my town. For some people Brickington is just another de-
> veloping town but, for me, it's wonderful. The old historical
> town centre, lined with traditional red brick housing and the
> church and the cobbled pavements, it makes you feel a sense of
> attachment…it just makes me feel happier.

Both Deborah and Julie's accounts demonstrate an affinity to Brickington
defined and valued through a discourse of 'red brick' architecture. The spatial
entity of red brick buildings works as a symbol of attachment and belonging.
Consider for example Julie's description of the historical town centre as 'wonderful'. Julie talks about the beauty of the red brick housing and the church
providing her with a sense of attachment. In these accounts, it is the spatial
entities that are directly selected and drawn on to describe and construct
Brickington identity. In other words, for Julie, it is the view of traditional
buildings and fields amongst other sights which are appreciated and sought
as a reminder of what life in Brickington is supposed to be.

There was also a sense of time coming through the accounts of some residents interviewed regarding the rural nature of Brickington identity. This was
mainly measured by the seasons and how these make the landscape alter.
Jane, for instance, talks about plants and the return and growing of plants in
the springtime in Brickington:

> The spring is a wonderful time of year in Brickington. The fields
> are bursting to life with new flowers, plants and trees. This is
> what really provides me with a sense of Brickingtonness.

Likewise, Barbara articulated:

> 'it was the fields, we're surrounded by fields. You've only got to
> go a few yards and you'll be in one. Even with the building that
> have gone on since we first arrived here, which has spread the

town out, but we still only have to go a very little way and you'll be in a field'.

The citing of plants, fields, and trees in this way to construct a particular rural identity is not surprising – there is, of course, a long history of trees and plants signifying spaces and the rural way of life, and its complex relationship between the social (people) and the spatial (trees and plants) - as Mabey (2007: 152) suggests: 'plants are part of what makes a locality, differentiates it, makes an amorphous site into place, a territory, an address'. Cloke and Jones (2001) highlight that trees and plants not only makes the place but is a marker of the temporal dimension of a place which people engage with over time. Brickington identity, therefore, becomes a performed identity, performed by things and people, and the way residents mark and map it through what they do, through the recursiveness of their experiences such as the sights of the fields as they walk in and around the town.

What is also interestingly imperative in the narratives of some residents' construction of Brickington identity was the length of time spent living in the town. Deborah, for instance, talked about how:

> Brickington has this included middle hub. I suppose in the older days when I was a kid, my dad was very much central to that with the council members. We've got Julie now who's very much the head; I know you've spoken to her. She seems to be the central lynchpin at the moment...we're the ones who have lived here all our lives so of course we see the red brick centre it makes us feel some sort of belonging to the town.

This is echoed by Kris:

> amongst the old 'Brickington Families' we kinda know each other because we've been here for generations and so there's a mutual but not necessarily deserved respect between us; even across the social strata solely based on attachment and belonging to the town and its red brick character surrounded by countryside.

These remarks from Deborah and Kris reflect what Cloke and Jones (2001: 654) call 'the recognition of time-deepened experience...the richest of sociality over time'. This means place attachment and identity which are developed, constructed and sustained by the longevity of residency - in other words, the longer you live in a place the greater your attachment and sense of identity. This can be seen in Deborah's remarks below:

because I'm from a lifelong family of the town and I know the history of the area. I like to go to the museum, and have a look around and then into the library and go through the archives. It's that sort of thing that creates a sense of belonging.

Brickington's rural character, in this context, is a product of structuration (Giddens, 1984) - that is, the combining effects of the physical landscape and people's associations given to the landscape are used to form an 'architecture' around which to construct its identity. Within this structurated understanding, the spatial markers of Brickington – e.g., trees, fields, farms, red brick buildings – become shorthand for its specific rural identity which, in turn, becomes structured as such because of the associations residents give it. Examples of this emerged from the interviews conducted with Deborah and Barbara:

> *Deborah:* There is a definite sense of rural nature here. Life in Brickington is a clear reflection of a traditional country town; peaceful, timely and surrounded by rolling hills, features typical of the English countryside.

> *Barbara:* Brickington is a very nice place to live. Other than that I think it makes for a slightly slower pace of life (than urban living). And I think going back to this idea of rural nature, I think it is representational of the countryside: beautiful fields and farmland and a lovely town centre.

These combining effects of the social and the spatial articulated by the residents in the quotations above reflect a wider 'cultural politics' (Harvey, 1996: 320) of Brickington identity, one that Harvey (1996: 320) refers to as a reflection of an 'institutionalised locus of social power'. Brickington identity, therefore, is not the two-dimensional conceptualisation of community identity that Amit and Rapport (2002) would have us believe. True, Brickington identity is constructed by the shared experiences of those residents with longer-standing in the town, but such shared social collectivities reinforced oppositional boundaries. For instance, shorter-term residents expressed less attachment to Brickington identity. This can be seen in the way Bobby talked about his lack of connection to the area:

> *Bobby:* Possibly, my lack of attachment to Brickington is because I work long hours, and have no interaction with the town. I'd suppose those who've lived in Brickington for generations

would have greater belonging and attachment to the town because of more involvement in local issues and concerns.

However, residents' sense of attachment and belonging to Brickington identity were far more complex than the juxtaposition between those who belong and those who do not. Much like Strathern's (1982) study of Elmdon (see Chapter 3 for more details), Brickington was stratified into three broad groups of belonging: residents who were born and raised in Brickington, residents who have lived in the town for fifteen, twenty years, and residents who have moved in on the back of social change (both nationally and internationally). The cultural use of red brick, plants and trees as a shorthand for Brickington identity, therefore, was dependent on the longevity of the resident and their 'discursive construction of affective loyalties' (Harvey, 1996: 323) to Brickington identity: that is, Brickington identity is given its ruralised meaning through the ways residents with greater attachment talked up the unique physical character of the area as 'rural' and the affective and emotional feelings it provides. The reiteration of Brickington identity, in turn, became a locational response to social and spatial change which reinforced the construction of boundaries. Harvey (1996) would characterise such a response as a 'reactionary' need for security of place, one that is often framed in terms of local distinctiveness or anchored in heritage-based expressions of 'rootedness' and 'authenticity'. Thus, using Harvey's analysis, the emphasis on red brick architecture and Brickington's proximity to fields and farmland, meant Brickington identity could act as a cultural response against an implicit threat of social and spatial change to its specific rural identity (Harvey, 1996: 294).

Social and physical threats to Brickington identity

This section will begin to explore the social and physical changes in Brickington that have contributed to the perceived loss of Brickington identity. According to Giddens (1991), threats do not tend to occur outside of an individual's social reality. Instead, they are internally formed as a response to specific situational phenomena. As a result, these internally produced threats give rise to feelings of anxiety which, as Giddens (1991: 44), suggests 'become pinned to items, traits or situations which have an oblique (although unconsciously precise) reaction to whatever originally provoked it'. This definition means that there is no need for a 'palpable threat' to Brickington identity, such as war, to effectively conjure up Brickington identity as precarious and perilously threatened. Concerns about loss of identity highlighted in the following sections resulted from a more complex, internally formed argument of protecting vested interests.

'Brickington was once a small village'

The expansion of housing was cited as a cause for concern by some residents. For example, Joseph explained:

> 'I wouldn't regard the modern state of Brickington as rural. I think it has lost its rural nature. And that started, as I've said, when the retail enterprises opened up and brought in new groups of people. I mean, just look at what Brickington is like now. It is mostly made up of new estates – run down estates – that have had to been developed to accommodate the influx of residents coming into the town.

Kris provided a similar response:

> Brickington was once a small village where the majority of buildings and houses were red brick or locally made stone. Now, with the rise of population and increase in housing developmentments you have buildings and houses that look completely out of character. I mean the newer housing development have homes made from white concrete next to ones made from yellow stone so the design and look of those has definitely changed. And with government plans to build another 1500 homes here it will get worse; the identity of the place (whatever's left) will be erased. It also takes away the rural nature about the place. Traditionally, English country homes all looked similar and in a way promoted an idea of what living in the country was like, and that was no different in Brickington. Now though, you've got so many out of character buildings it doesn't reflect this.

What came out of these interviews was a sense of anxiety about the decline of a traditional rural community which derived from the increase in houses being built and the effect this was having on the rural character of Brickington. When questioned what was it about the increase of housing that had an impact on the rural nature of Brickington, several residents mentioned the design of the buildings as being out of character. For instance, Julie, Irvin, and Kris all talked very passionately about changes in the local architecture:

> *Julie:* Brickington has become urban sprawl! Housing is spreading out and using up all the countryside. We've had new housing estates built along the southern side of town and that looks

dreadful - they're very close together, the roads are really narrow and it hasn't worked. It's awful and really upsetting

Kris: Well, there was a failure to address the London overspill back in the 1980s. You see, the town was asked if planners and developers could build more homes for people from London to live in because the city was getting crowded. The 'Brickington Families' at the time said no but what happened is that Brickington got this overspill and growth anyway because the government at the time, and you've gotta remember this was during Thatcher's 'right to buy' scheme, decided to develop housing anyway and what you got were houses that look higgly piggley and out of character with the rest of the town. And so, the housing developments and the boom that has hit Brickington since has had a negative impact on the town. Certainly in terms of the types of structures and density of houses, the lack of thought on traditional infrastructure in Brickington and that sorta thing.

Irvin: You are surrounded by crap! Some of the shops on the High Street don't look very traditional; ugly white concrete looking things. The new housing developments have a mishmash of design from hideous yellow reconstituted stone to brown brick and they look dreadful. There is no sense of Brickington heritage at all and is one of the reasons why I'm part of the planning team. We need to reinstall Brickingtonness back into the town.

Correspondingly, Joseph also spoke about the types of people these new developments had brought in which affected the rural character of Brickington:

Ever since the increase of housing, new groups of people have arrived. We can see this on the new estates where people don't really talk; there are skips on front lawns and graffiti along the walls and garages. People don't have the pride that they once did. These people do not reflect the Brickington community.

Nevertheless, despite this perceived threat of loss of character many of the residents interviewed also talked about the importance of generational kinships in Brickington. This idea of generational kinship and living locally was important for Kris: 'I met my wife locally. I brought my children up in this area, and they went to school here', he continues: 'I think living locally is incredibly important in places like Brickington, especially amongst the old 'Brickington Families' as we know each other'.

Such perceived threats of loss of character, therefore, may not be fully justified. If residents tend to live locally and socially reproduce the values of the locality, then it is most likely the physically changing nature of Brickington is a response to local population growth. This is supported in the wider literature (see, for example, Gallent and Robinson, 2011), which has identified it was most often than not the growth of local village communities which gave rise to increased housing and not necessarily from an in-migration from the outside. Therefore, such attitudes in Brickington to protect its 'traditional' values, customs and norms were mostly ones created through a 'village of the mind' (Pahl, 1966) which become 'real' when local identity is perceived to be threatened. There was evidence of this in how residents talked about the rumours of a McDonalds store opening up on the High Street.

Rumours of McDonalds

> *Kris:* Before the overspill from London we had independent retailers, bakers, butchers all on the High Street and it was thriving. The population surges and people move in so places like Waitrose buy land and open. And because these people from London and other newcomers see Waitrose and recognise it they'll go there. This has had a huge impact because local business can't afford to run a shop anymore and it's a pity because rural life is supposed to be about individualism of the High Street, now we are getting to look more and more like everywhere else.

Underlying Kris's disapproval of the rise of service-industry was a fear of the changing rural aesthetic of Brickington's High Street. He grew up in Brickington where independent retailers formed a significant aspect of rural life in the town, similar to the importance of farming Sarsby (1997) found in her study of rural Devon. Loss of the 'traditional' rural High Street has been linked to ontological insecurity. In his study of rural imagining in Cornwall, Philips (2008) identified that local residents placed the High Street at the centre of village life. According to Philips (2008: 139), the High Street embodied what country life should be: a chocolate-box community occupied with quaint buildings and filled with people pleasantly talking to each other. The main thrust of Philips's (2008: 130) argument is that such a picture projected 'rural imagining'; that is, it only existed outside of the collective minds of the village because local residents extended some effort into romanticising the past to seek shelter from a future of change and uncertainty.

When rumour of a McDonald's store was opening up in Brickington, some residents expressed feelings of abjection. 'I think it'll encourage more and more families from London to move to Brickington, Jane said. 'It'll also bring mess and litter and make Brickington more city-like'. When further questioned what it was about McDonalds that would make Brickington increasingly 'city-like', Jane responded:

> Well when I think about McDonalds, I immediately think of cheap, bland food which is the same everywhere you go and people eating there because they're just too busy to cook. It just reminds me of big cities where things tend to be the same and people live much busier lives than in the country.

Likewise, Danielle spoke very passionately about the detrimental impact service-industry is having on Brickington's rural identity:

> I think change is detrimental to rural community because there is less individuality on the High Street and, in my mind, rural communities have this individuality, eccentricity and the like of the different on the High Street. But now, you've got big brand stores which attract a lot of people from the city and job opportunities which attract a lot of Polish. It feels as though our rural heritage is being threatened.

The inclusion of McDonalds on the High Street and the concern expressed by some residents around the decline of Brickington identity are reflected in the wider literature around McDonaldisation (Ritzer, 1993). McDonaldisation is defined as 'the [bureaucratic] process by which the principles of the fast-food restaurant are coming to dominate more and more sectors of American society as well as the rest of the world' (Ritzer, 1993: 1). According to Ritzer, McDonaldised institutes operate in accordance with four principles: calculability, efficiency, control, and predictability. It is the concept of predictability which is important in this context as it refers to the idea that no matter where someone goes they can expect the same service. A similar process is happening through standardising and homogenising of everyday life as a result of change where people are beginning to associate the place with the familiar (Ritzer 1993), and any sense of individual/community identity is lost.

Thus, although people have the desire for the timely and tranquil environment of the English countryside, they will only do so if it offers them familiarity as well. For instance, Irvin reminisced: 'me and my wife always wanted to live in the country and when we were looking to move out of our house in London and saw Brickington we thought "wow!"….having a Waitrose in the town really attracted us to the area'. When prompting Irvin further on whether such amenities affected the sense of 'rurality' about Brickington he articulated:

> No, I wouldn't have said so. I do get a feeling that the lifelong folk of the town resent them but, Brickington, to my wife and I has always been rural. The countryside isn't defined by how many shops a town has, but rather the beauty that exists in and around it. For example, you are minutes away from open fields and to me that is what country living all is about.

Reflected in the above quotation is that, unlike other residents who have perhaps lived in Brickington for generations, or twenty, thirty years, who see its rural nature changing and eroding, residents such as Irvin do not have an issue with service-industry, instead of seeing it as a positive attribute to rural life. This can be seen in Jake's remarks regarding the increase of service-industry in Brickington: 'I don't mind shops like Asda or Costa coming into the town. For me, I can see the potential in it for jobs as long as it is done sensibly and they don't rush businesses in it shouldn't harm the place's rural nature'. What these narratives demonstrate is the local tensions which put a strain on the cohesive rural identity of Brickington: another threat.

Competing interests

The strain on a collective Brickington identity was evident in the different conversations I had with residents. Some spoke of the loss of rural community which directly related to globalised change and the decline of local social interaction, values, and customs in the town, whilst others discussed the convenience of change. Both Foucault's (1986) concept of *heterotopia* and Lefebvre's (1991) concept of *lived space* are helpful here in analysing the competing ways in which residents talked about the change in Brickington. For Lefebvre, 'lived space' is the space of 'possibilities and perils' (Soja, 1985: 68); it refers to the space that is struggled over and within; space where identities are maintained, resisted, and change occurs (Lefebvre, 1991; Soja, 1985). While, for Foucault (1986: 24-25), heterotopia was definable as 'the curious property of being in relation with all other sites but in such a way as to suspect, neutralise or invert the set of relations that they happen to designate, mirror or reflect...[heterotopia] juxtaposes in a single real space several spaces, several sites that are themselves incompatible'.

The notion of a plurality of sites where different forms of ordering take place but, which are at the same time contained within a particular space (such as Brickington) is one that is relevant for interpreting the different ways resident talked about change. Take, for example, the narratives Deborah and Julie provided around the loss of traditional values and customs:

> *Deborah:* When I was little you'd go to the butcher, you'd go to the fish monger, you had a chat with the fish monger, he knew what you liked he put it in the bag as you walked in the door. Then you went to go and get your bread and there were three shops selling fresh bread, and that formed the basis of all social relationships in the town because in order to get your household shop you'd interact with loads of different people. Now, you go to Waitrose or Asda, and you interact with one and you don't really have a conversation with them. You are there to do your shopping and that's it. I mean there are independent shops which I do use but it's not like it once was and this is what the Town Team are trying to bring back.

> *Julie:* Brickington did have a high sense of community and belonging. People really get involved and offered to help out, particularly around Christmas time where we organised a dinner for the elderly who are alone that time of year. Seeing people do that outta the goodness of their own heart on Christmas day was fantastic and that provided me with a sense of community, a sense of a rural community. But you do not have that anymore. There are less and less people on the High Street. They'd rather go to the local Asda, or the local Waitrose and not talk to one another in the town.

Now, compare this to the way Bobby and Marc talked about the convenience of change in Brickington:

> *Bobby:* For me personally, I think a bit of convenience is good. I mean, I remember when I first moved to this town. I was working long hours and fancied a bottle of wine. But, at six in the evening in Brickington, back then, you couldn't have got that. But now, with Waitrose and what have you, you can and it's convenient.

> *Marc:* I like Costa but; as a whole, but people feel quite negatively to it. This is because putting in a big business takes away the small businesses. But, for me personally, I enjoy the convenience of having the likes of Costa, Asda and Waitrose. Costa's

aim is to make money and if it can do that and benefit the town
then so be it.

There is an apparent juxtaposition in the quotations cited above: a juxtaposition which demonstrates a valuing of Brickington space contingent upon
where people stand and their claims to belonging and attachment to the
community. Deborah's reflections on local shopping habits of the past as the
basis for the formation of social relationships depicts a person with a higher
vested interest, a longer-standing and an attachment to Brickington. This is
evident as she is able to recall, recollect and romanticise the past as a way to
justify the negative consequences of development in the area. Conversely, if
we examine the remarks made by Bobby about the convenience of supermar-
kets in the town, we can see the case of someone who has relatively recently
moved into Brickington and is, therefore, less invested and less attached to
the area. This lack of vested interest in Brickington results in his expression of
positivity towards development. A similar juxtaposition of opinions has been
made by other rural scholars around discourses of crime in the English countryside. In Yarwood and Gardner's (2000: 405) study, for instance, some residents perceived smuggling and poaching as transgressive, but for others, it
was things like raves and trespass.

In this context, there is a paradoxical nature of Brickington: a place conceived on the one hand as a site of reluctance to change; whilst on the other, a
place that is accepting of it. However, despite such competing interests expressed by residents, there was mutual compatibility between the two opposing perspectives. Hetherington (1997) calls for scrutiny of the social ordering
of everyday life, and in many ways, while the rural social order of Brickington
revealed tensions and competing interests among residents, their juxtaposed
position gave way to a coherent ordering of the town. The desire for tradition
and opposing change can all be accommodated in one narrative as long as
they involve populations who embrace change and difference. Nevertheless,
the residents of Brickington who opposed change (those with middle-class
status and long standing in the town) tended to latch onto the past ideals,
traditions, and customs of the town as a way of maintaining a particular local
identity. One example of this is the local carnival, and in the section below, I
provide a detailed examination of the event and how both the social and the
spatial are produced and reproduced to maintain and reinforce a specific
rural identity perceived to be perilously threatened.

A night at the carnival

Carnivals often display localised rituals - oft-repeated actions that are routinely followed in order to represent a certain image. These ritual-like routines

become associated with social identity in which they distinguish certain characteristics and functions of community life. Ziakas and Boukas (2013: 98) have suggested that celebrations – for instance, through the means of a procession - is a form of civic ritual where 'all normal business is interrupted for the parade: streets are decorated in exceptional ways, costumes of parade participants are specially designed, and music is publicly played'. Together with the mammoth crowds that gather in the parade grounds, along with the streets or at vantage points, the atmosphere is transformed into an emotive one. Carnival rituals are also 'potentially a period of exaggeration of the central values and axioms of the culture in which it occurs' (Turner, 1974: 154). Indeed, Turner's view is important here because she suggests that 'the study of carnival rituals [is] the key to an understanding of the constitution of social identity'. Often, it is argued that the values that rituals reveal and emphasise are shared values (Ziakas and Boukas, 2013) since collective participation in rituals suggests affirmation of those values being celebrated.

Apart from the links with local community values, another related characteristic of carnivals is their inextricable link to social relations. In particular, Marston (1989: 255) maintains that parades, as a specific form of carnival ritual, are 'complex commentaries' on social relations. They 'are both shaped by the field of power relations in which they take place, and are used to act on and influence those relations' (Davis, 1986: 6). This is possible because, as Davis (1986: 6) goes on to maintain 'in them performers define who can be a social actor and what subjects and ideas are available for communication and consideration. These defining images, in turn, shape the actions and alternatives people can imagine and propose'.

A specific example of the link between carnival rituals, such as processions and social relations is the way in which these rituals reinforce dominant group cohesion. In other words, by emphasising the common attributes of identity or ways of being (Ziakas and Boukas, 2013), carnivals can emphasise the shared values of particular social groups/communities (Bocock, 1974) by demonstrating community power and solidarity (Marston, 1989). It is this celebration of togetherness which is especially important in a fragmented world or a world where tolerance of difference is, at least, treading a precariously thin line as it provides belonging which the contemporary social world is increasingly unlikely to give (Bauman, 2001).

Another characteristic of the ritual of the carnival is its role in sustaining a sense of place. Connerton (1989) argues that ritual performances of carnivals are important in building up collective memory, which is in turn crucial for the development of a sense of home. Carnivals are characterised by a high degree of display and theatrics (e.g., lights, parades, music, cheering) (Daniels and Cosgrove, 1993: 58). As a landscape metaphor, carnivals impress not so much by their actual substance but through their pageantry and fanfare. Such spectacles are designed to create a sense of an actual social identity and feelings of belonging and togetherness through the use of awe and wonder. This may be attained through the use of specific images on floats; the creation of occasion and circumstances for celebration; and visual effects (Ley and Olds, 1988; Kearns, 1993; Yeoh and Lau., 1995), and it is these spectacles created during carnival time that pervade the whole of social life, invading the realms of people's practical consciousness (Debord, 1973); or to put it another way, the actions people do but which they cannot articulate.

The Brickington carnival

The carnival was held along the Historic Town Centre and Albury: an area made up of narrow streets surrounded by red brick buildings and traditional thatched cottages tucked away behind the local church on one side and open green space in between traditional, independent shops erected from the coarse rubble with brick dressing on the other. Moreover, there was open green space where the fun fair was positioned and was adjoined by the frontages of properties in the Square on the left side, and on the right, it was overlooked by the roundabout leading towards the centre of the High Street and the southern end of town. The fun fair area was laid with grass, except for an area of paved slabs at the back of the field which had been placed to allow access to the public bridge footpath which joined to the local Waitrose supermarket (see Figure 5.4).

According to local archives, the history of the carnival can be traced back to 1918 just after the end-of-war celebrations. Its purpose was to welcome back soldiers from the First World War and to help resettle them into local life. Its success meant an annual event should be held called 'carnival' to celebrate local life, and the support of local organisations and residents of the town were soon enlisted. While the event has been running in Brickington for a century, it is only very recently that it has gained traction amongst long-term residents who articulated that they needed it because they were proud of the town and its character and that this needed to be celebrated. This was best captured by Julie, who passionately said: 'my family run their calendar in their minds, and when we get carnival there is such excitement in our household. We are very Brickington born and bred so it's great to see floats and activities that represent the town'.

Figure 5.4 – The Brickington carnival

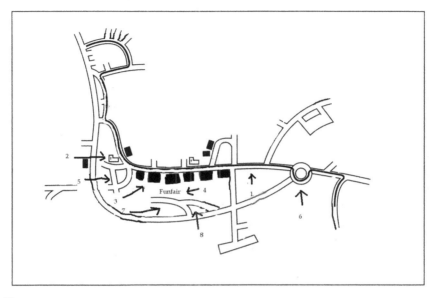

Key

■■■■■ Procession route

1. The High Street
2. Thatched cottages
3. Independent shops
4. Funfair

5. The Square
6. Roundabout
7. Public footpath
8. Waitrose

Author's own

Danielle also commented on how the carnival is reflective of her attachment to the town: 'the carnival really makes me feel a connection to the town. The experience of seeing floats that represent local industries is really something special; it paints a picture of times gone by that I still remember fondly'. Likewise, other residents expressed the importance of the carnival. Steven, for instance, highlighted: 'the carnival is truly representative of Brickington. It is about celebrating the place in which we live and views of the countryside'. Bobby agreed, 'Well, the carnival is supposed to represent Brickington as a rural town. We have a parade every year with floats depicting periods of the history of Brickington; it's very celebratory'. What these comments demonstrate is that the carnival helps to maintain these atmospherically feelings of Brickington identity which, in turn, is facilitated by the attachment and sense of belonging of some its residents. In the sections below, I illustrate how the experience and organisation of the Brickington carnival helped reconstruct a particular local identity. This is done by examining the influence of spectacle and ritual of the procession on some residents' perceptions of Brickington's rural identity and how the organisation of the carnival by those with longer-standing in the town helped maintain and reinforce Brickington's rural character.

The carnival procession

I arrived at the High Street and took my place as a spectator of the procession at 6.50pm, ten minutes before the parade started. There was an atmosphere of exhilaration and thrill running through the High Street as residents gathered, laughing and talking to one another as they waited for the procession to begin. At 7 pm the procession made its way from the bottom of the High Street and wound its way up to the thickly populated Square, cheered by residents to images and sounds of steam engines and floats. Residents were crowding along the roadside outside of the funfair and waving and cheering from windows of the block of flats that sat just left of Kings Street. The first collection of floats comprised steam engines and a float depicting a brick maker in blue overalls chipping away at a workbench, crafting the red brick which characterises the houses that lay in the Historic Town Centre. The float had an illuminous sign above it saying 'Brickington brick industry'. The use of steam engines and the pageantry of celebrating old, local industries tended to reinforce the effects of creating a particular local identity by invading the spaces of everyday life and transforming ordinary streets into, what Goheen (cited in O'Leary, 2012: 11) calls the 'symbolic capture of local life'. Here the ceremonial landscape combined with the habitation of local people influenced how some residents perceived Brickington's rural identity.

The second segment of floats arrived between 7.10pm and 7.20pm. There consisted a marching band and floats designed by the local school children. In form and composition, these floats offered a glimpse of what the children thought were the best features about life in Brickington. One float, in particular, was a constructed replica of The Square, depicting the medieval church made from paper-maché and painted grey. The church was the main feature of the float; standing in the centre with a painted backdrop of the red brick buildings that made the centre of town distinct behind it and the children were dressed up as townsfolk from the early 19th century; huddled in a group and engaged in chatter. The imagery of a group of residents talking outside of the church is doing something particular here: it is playing out a social drama. The carnival under this context became a symbolic battle, a clash of competing identities in which by 'showing off' the residents with longer-standing witnesses itself as a whole, whilst simultaneously restraining the celebratory moods of those individuals who were positioned as the 'out-group' of the community, or those who do not belong within the boundaries of Brickington identity. The transgressive spirit of Brickington carnival allowed residents to assert their identity symbolically in a permissive space, where the grotes-query, juxtaposition, chaos, and clash of symbols and practices are a reflec-tion of the diversity of values and vocabularies held by people-in-place. This is best seen in my field note depicting the dynamics of people watching the procession:

> The crowd gathering to watch the parade is massive, possibly in its thousands: an estimate Julie provided me but which I thought she overstated. The marching band is coming through. There is a cacophony of noise: music and sounds of people cheering and clapping. The group who appear to be the loudest could possibly be those with attachment to the local area. The atmosphere is split between those who actively chanting and cheering and those who are more passive, or ambivalent to-wards the event. Could these possibly be newcomers? It is hard to tell, but next to me are a Polish couple speaking in Polish quietly to each other and disengaged with what is happening so my observations may present some credibility.

> (Field note from the Brickington Carnival, 5/10/13)

The carnival procession, therefore, may act as a cultural container for the enactment of social dramas, something which is seized upon by those mid-dle-class residents with longer-standing and greater attachment as an oppor-tunity to demonstrate a system of power: a system where such rural imagery attempts to draw connections with a momentous past. This is what Gilroy (2005) calls *'postcolonial melancholia'*: the ability to deny social change as a way to emphasise and romanticise the past.

Gilroy's (2005) *'postcolonial melancholia'* can be seen in the last segment of the parade which occurred from 7.30pm to its end at 8pm. During this time the floats all resembled natural elements of the countryside. One float that stood out consisted of a painted backdrop of rolling green fields and paper shrubs and hedgerows in the forefront of the float. On the far right was a tree crafted from brown painted cardboard rolls with green paper-machéd leaves. In the centre was a golden spray-painted chair representing a throne in which the carnival queen sat, dressed in white with daisies and wildlife around her. Such images of nature could be interpreted as attempting to represent 'the spirit of the countryside' (Holloway, 2004: 54) by celebrating the rural charac-ter of Brickington – e.g., rolling greens, hedgerows, and so on. This rural im-agery is significant in contributing to the maintenance of Brickington's local identity in times of uncertainty (Gibson and Connell, 2011). The demonstrations and deliberate use of scenes, along with specific sounds and music of marching bands I observed during the procession all combined to construct a certain way of capturing Brickington identity and can be seen in the way participants talked about the importance of these ideals. This was perhaps best captured by Deborah who said:

> Brickington was a lot different when I was growing up. Everybody knew everybody and so everybody knew. You could walk up the High Street and talk to anyone. But I don't think this is quite as evident although it is still here to a certain extent. So from that aspect it's changed; and it's a shame really because things were much nicer then.

Social networks and maintaining local identity

Physical displays of identity are not without an element of the social. People are integrated into the constitution of spaces (Hiller and Hanson, 1993). The ordering of individuals in relation to each other is constitutionally contingent on space, and dependent on their social relationship. People are positioned by the actions and practices of others, and they also actively position themselves. But this active positioning is not 'active' in the sense there is some sort of cognitive reasoning for action, but rather these actions are located in the practical consciousness (Giddens, 1984) of people: it is embedded in the values, customs, and traditions of the locality. Thus, space only has some sort of structural property or purpose because of its relational ordering by individuals.

Before space can be ordered, however, it must be given some sort of meaning. Meaning is generally defined as the 'individual signification or the internal symbolisation, representation, and conceptualisation of the external world' (Gergen, 1994: 19). Thus the Brickington carnival - including all residents' feelings, thoughts, and experiences as well as the subsequent sense of rurality that some residents expressed from their participation in, or attendance - may be the consequence of the performances that were organised by those longer-standing residents in the area. In November 2014 I sat in on one of the organisational meetings held by the carnival committee, after being invited by Bobby a year prior. The committee meets four times throughout the year in order to prepare for the following year's carnival celebrations. Some members of the committee – e.g., Julie, Jane, and Susan - I recognised from previous research interviews. The aim of the meeting was to talk through what went well that year and what could be done to improve the experience the following year. Towards the latter half of the meeting Martha, very cogently suggested:

> For next year I think the carnival should have a theme. So far it's been a mismatch of these different floats. I do think people would appreciate where they're living a lot more if you showed off an hour long display of floats representing the rural side of Brickington, amongst this new building work that's going on in the southern end of town.

Susan liked the idea and agreed with Marta:

> That's a really good idea. Over the past couple of years we've had Party on the Meadow, Party at the Rec and the Street Party for the Queen's diamond jubilee and this has helped boost our identity as a town. Continuing to promote images of Brickington during the parade will help maintain this identity.

The committee concluded that for the next year's carnival festivities the procession would be dedicated to Brickington's architecture. The rationale being that it had been thirty years since the closure of Brickington brick industry and two hundred years since its induction as the staple building material of the area. After deciding on a theme, the conversation of the meeting quickly turned to how this might be represented in the parade. Irene suggested 'we should get everyone to contribute a float dedicated to particular area of Brickington', while Julie thought it would be a good idea to have floats telling the history of Brickington's local character: 'We should arrange the floats, so it tells the story of Brickington's historic building, from the building of the church in the 14th century to present day'.

What the data is suggesting here is that the construction of the carnival and its effective and emotional associations with a particular rural identity is based on *event dramaturgy*. Taken from Goffman's (1999 – originally published in 1959) notion of dramaturgy as a way of explaining social behaviour as forms of rituals and social dramas, Ziakas and Costa (2012: 32) define *event dramaturgy* as 'the extraction of shared meanings enabled by the projection and/or performance of symbolic representations in an event's activities'. Thus the effective and emotional attachments felt and expressed by those longer-term residents during the Brickington carnival only had an impact because of the symbols the same group of individuals used to organise the procession and funfair activities, which was also an attempt to reinstate a flagging loss of a particular set of rural values, customs, and traditions:

> *Julie:* The carnival makes me feel very rural. When I think of rural life – and this is silly – I think of people idly chatting away, being involved within your community, and rows of thatched cottages. So, yes I do think the carnival is very rural in that sense. When you attend you will bump into someone you know and the position of it is right in the centre so, if the red brick buildings in the background you have this oldie worldy sort of look to the event. And it's this type of thing about the carnival that makes me proud to live in Brickington.

> *Kris:* The carnival is truly a reflection of traditional rural values. During carnival time it feels as though everyone comes out to cheer Brickington and in a way, Englishness. At the carnival you'll see everybody chatting and being happy; these are English values. The fact that everybody knows everybody else and they're here to celebrate these values – now that's English - I don't think you'll see this type of thing in carnivals in any other country. And I think these traditional values demonstrated through the carnival are typical of the residents of Brickington, particularly the ones like myself who have been here for generations.

Using Giddens' (1984) structuration theory, we can see that social practices cannot be separated from the places that surround them, and as Sheller and Urry (2004: 1) maintain '...actions inform place, shape the places where actions are performed, and drive the making and unmaking of place-based activities'. Thus, social identity may be an outcome of the *relationality* of the performance, where *relationality* refers to and includes open-ended interactions through which social identity emerges out and becomes structured (Dillon, 2014). It was, therefore, the residents with a greater attachment that perceived themselves to be 'guardians' of Brickington identity and so used the carnival as a means to produce, reproduce and maintain a particular rural identity from wider pressures of globalised social and spatial change.

Conclusion

In this chapter, I have explored the threats to Brickington identity. The narratives in the data cited suggested there was – by and large – a shared concern amongst some residents about the erosion of Brickington identity. These threats were primarily positioned around the loss of a particular rural identity, including housing growth, the rise of the service industry and competing vested interests which mainly led to a perception of a 'threatened community'.

What the data in this chapter has also outlined is that, in a roundabout way, a threatened Brickington identity from wider pressures of change gave rise to desires to maintain local identity. The maintenance of a particular rural identity was very much at the heart of the Brickington carnival: theatrical display of the procession promoted a particular local identity through the representation of local history, which was simultaneously instilled by the local carnival committee. Members of the carnival committee saw themselves as guardians of Brickington identity, and this provided the physical, theatrical demonstration with meaning by deciding what should and should not be displayed. However, longer-term residents did not only seek to maintain the rural character of Brickington, but they also attempted to control the town's particular rural identity. It is this controlling of Brickington identity that the next chapter now turns to.

Chapter 6

Looking rural, being rural, talking rural: Informal social control and protecting local rural identity from social change

Introduction

The following chapter sets out how long-term residents enacted informal social control in Brickington and how notions of rurality were created through individuals' routines and actions. The first part of this chapter draws upon participant and direct observational data that allowed for the observation of informal social control in practice: that is, the way in which long-term residents acted out a Brickington rural identity through their everyday routine activities. This discussion provides an analysis of how Brickington's identity of being 'rural' was being passively protected through the enactment of structural, ideological and cultural controls. This first section achieves this by offering an in-depth account of these types of informal social control operating in the town through my participant and direct observations of *811 Coffee*, the St. Peters craft fair and market and whilst on the High Street.

The second half of this chapter turns to explore the 'active' community controls enacted in Brickington. Some of the long-term residents who took part in this study were members of the Brickington Neighbourhood Planning Group (BNPG), which were designing a Neighbourhood Plan as a response to an inappropriate building development that they felt was eroding Brickington's rural identity. Following Black's (1976) argument that informal social control needs to be understood more widely as focusing on socially problematic behaviour as opposed to just crime management, this section explores how Brickington's rural identity is actively protected through the Neighbourhood Plan. The analysis demonstrates how community action to protect the rural character of Brickington from an in-appropriate building development led to the enactment of community controls which were used to reinforce and protect Brickington's rural character despite the changing landscape of the place. Ultimately, through an analysis of informal social control and its operation within Brickington, this chapter demonstrates how the concept of 'rurality' is protected and reinforced through individuals' activities and actions. I will make claim that similar to Brexit and notions of Britishness (see Chapter 2), informal social control also works in a 'beyond crime management' way to understand the ways in which rural identities are protected and maintained against wider threats of social change.

Looking rural, being rural, talking rural

There is a general perception amongst rural communities that social and spatial change has – by and large - facilitated the diminution of the rural community as an indicator of identity and differentiation and replaced it by processes of individualisation. Giddens (1991) argues that individualisation is part of the process of globalisation in which social relations are becoming disembedded from local contexts and re-articulated across wide time-space distances. This is supported by Massey (1994: 162) who suggests that as 'social relations which constitute a locality increasingly stretch beyond its borders; less and less of these relations are constrained within the place itself'.

However, as I have articulated in Chapter 3, the process of globalisation has not facilitated the demise of rural community but rather reinforced its emphasis as a 'secure territory' (Allan and Crow, 1989: 7), a 'refuge' or 'sanctuary' (Jackson, 1991: 34), or a physical and psychological shelter (Dupuis and Thorns, 1998; Saunders, 1990) from the uncertainties of change. This focus on rural community as a 'refuge' from change has an impact on informal social control in a particular way. It causes the adoption of routines as coping mechanisms to provide ontological security against unwarranted social change, ergo creating exclusionary rural community associations based on systems of governance (Giddens, 1991) where those with the greatest emotional or psychological investment in community life construct themselves as guardians of place identity.

Within this analysis Giddens (1991) advocates that routines and habits serve as coping mechanisms for daily life because they imply ontological security. Routines, which are a predominant form of an individual's daily social activity, are linked psychologically to an individual's tacit attempt to maintain a sense of place and identity (Giddens, 1984; 1991). And, as I will go on to demonstrate in the sections below, routines were enacted passively to construct structural, ideological and cultural controls as a way to protect Brickington's rural identity from social change.

Americano, with a little cream

Community public spaces are significant examples of complex and diverse processes of place-making and identity construction within rural areas. They are places where the norms and values of rural communities are socially constructed and consumed. They are also places where structural, ideological and cultural controls are enacted through social interactions (Laurier and Philo, 2006; Zukin, 2010; Woldoff *et al.*, 2013). *811 Coffee* along the Station Street in the medieval industrial expansion area of the town is one such example where structural, ideological and cultural controls of Brickington's rural identity were passively enacted.

811 Coffee was a local business which offered a variety of coffee blends alongside a well-stocked fridge filled with pastries and other delicacies, a chromed Italian coffee machine and a blackboard menu that was hanged behind the till and was the de-facto place for social interaction for many residents in the town. I first became aware of the existence of 811 Coffee one afternoon in October 2013. Upon finding it, I decided to go in, have a coffee and conduct some participant observational work. On entering, I was greeted by a friendly gentleman who said 'Good afternoon, what coffee will you be having today'. My initial reaction was how my 'outsider' status could go unnoticed in a town whose residents had conferred to me a sense of wariness towards outsiders? Nevertheless, I responded by saying 'an Americano, with a little cream please' and took a seat in the corner of the shop on one of the round metal 'café style' tables to observe the comings and goings of local life.

What was apparent during my participant observations of *811 Coffee* and in my field notes is that the shop seemed to attract similar sorts of customers, individuals who seemed to have particular vested interests in the community and local life. The description of *811 Coffee* I made on 19/10/13 is a typical example of this lack of diversity in clientele:

> Three older women, coming in from the outside, are at the till ordering cappuccinos. They knew the shop owner by name, and asked him how he was and whether he'd been up to much lately before taking a seat on one of the leather sofas situated along the front windows of the shop. I took a sip of my coffee and from my table noticed an Asian man hesitating outside, deciding whether or not to come in, before walking by. Half-hour later, an elderly white (long-term residents?) couple came in. They ordered a blueberry muffin to share and sat next to the three women who entered earlier. I noticed the people knew each other and started talking amongst themselves.

> (Field note taken from 811 Coffee, 19/10/13)

Noticeable in this field account is not only the lack of cultural diversity of the shop's customers, but also how such lack of diversity facilitated a sociable nature of *811 Coffee* in which the residents who used this public space were passively constructing the shop as a site of retreatism and sociality against the ever-changing and individualised nature of Brickington. Such an analysis and observation is supported by Hall's (2012: 52) ethnography of 'Nick's Caff' in London in which she identified the cafe as 'a small meeting place representing a tradition in the middle of a large and rapidly changing city'.

By identifying 'Nick's Caff' as a site of social retreatism from the processes of change and diversity, Hall's work echoes the sustained emphasis by Zukin (2010) who asserts that public spaces have the ability to creates exclusionary identities. It is Zukin's (2010) notion of public spaces creating and sustaining an exclusionary identity that was most striking about my participant observations in *811 Coffee*. The environment (the music) and a sense of being at social comfort (chatting, laughter, banter) seemed to be get folded into wider processes of identity-making in which customers constructed themselves as 'rural'. This was noticeable from the conversations I could overhear from my table about farming activity and other local goings-on (e.g., 'I'm having to take the cattle to slaughter by myself tomorrow as the lads on the farm keep phoning in sick!' and 'I'll meet you in town tomorrow as I need some new cutlery. I wouldn't mind popping into Crocker's').

Such processes of sociality and rural identity construction amongst the mundanity or taken for granted encounters in *811 Coffee* created a space of notional exclusionary boundaries, and this was apparent when an Indian gentleman entered and ordered a drink:

> A man of Indian origin came in and ordered a latte to go. The guy behind the counter says 'Hi, I haven't seen you around Brickington before. Where are you from?' The customer responds by saying, 'Nowhere, I am from Brickington'.

> (Field note taken from 811 Coffee, 19/10/1)

What can be seen from the observational data highlighted above is that the processes of place-making and sociality by long-term residents within *811 Coffee* meant that difference got recognised, claimed and challenged as not being authentically Brickington or 'rural'. The challenging of difference, here, appears as banal and convivial rather than testing and sanctioning. This banal challenging of difference in *811 Coffee* works effectively with Goffman's (1963: 86) concept of civil inattention where inattention demands little more than social recognition and an unpanicked acknowledgement of the presence of diverse others within the boundaries of the setting to protect the structural, ideological and cultural norms of Brickington's rural identity through the everyday challenging of difference or non-normative practices and behaviours.

Rural crafts

Having discussed how structural, ideological and cultural controls were enacted by long-term residents at a local coffee shop in Brickington, I now want to explore how they were enacted in the iconography of the St. Peters craft fair and market, and the manner in such an event reinforced and reproduced an exclusive Brickington rural identity. The construction of a rural identity, using specific sets of symbols and symbolism were evidently central to the craft fair and market in enacting structural, ideological and cultural controls. Here the presence of particular crafts and delicacies, such as handmade wood jewellery cases, knitwear, and locally made treats, became facets of a broader picture; used as part of the construction of a rural identity within a town undergoing change. The display of such crafts transcended iconography, and the implications of the event were both psychological and corporeal in creating and sustaining a sense of 'rurality':

> Despite its size, the craft fair was bursting with active social life from residents. Loud roars of chatter between residents echoed the room. The place was packed with a variety of goods. There was handcrafted jewellery and personalised trinket boxes, next to crocheted and knitted baby clothes and alongside homemade jams, marmalade and cakes. The craft fair embodied a sense of a stereotypical rural life that I only had heard about in media programmes such as *the Archers*.

> (Field note taken from St. Peters craft fair and market, 1/11/13)

This enacted sense of 'rurality' that I experienced during the craft fair and market can be understood through what Poole (1997) calls the representation of a 'visual economy'. According to Poole, a visual economy is the way identities are created, maintained and protected by images that serve to organise people, ideas, and objects, and that this is achieved through the production of symbols by individuals; the circulation of such symbols amongst individuals; and the cultural resources and systems through which images are interpreted and valued. In addition to this, Campbell (2006: 5) asserts the idea of a visual economy is to make clear the visual field (rural identity) is both made possible by and a product of relations of power and that these power relations bear at least some relationship to wider social structures which are themselves associated with. The consequence of this, he argues, is that communities can be made up of people who are part of the same economy but not necessarily part of the same culture. The visual economy can, therefore, produce and promote cultural difference by invoking images that cannot be isolated as discrete objects but have to be understood as imbricated in networks of materials, institutions, markets, affects, cultural histories and social contexts. In short, the craft fair and market drew together the visual symbols of Brickington's rural identity that, not only served to perform Brickington as iconographically 'rural', but also facilitated the production of exclusive boundaries (Sibley, 1997).

Moreover, the visual presence of rurality at the craft fair and market that was evident through the thick sense of social interaction and the display of specific rural crafts and goods, such as ceramic pottery, local meat and treats, handmade ornaments and upcycled clothes and furniture, enacted particular structural, ideological and cultural controls. This meant that long-term residents could control difference by effectively managing Brickington's rural identity by making sure 'outsiders' comply with the norms and values of the event:

> Walking around the craft fair there was an obvious sense of rurality which was apparent throughout my participation at the event. The friendliness of the sellers, the passive chatter about daily life between people and the consumption of local goods and produce all added to this feeling of being part of rural life. While leisurely looking around the stalls, I noticed a couple of Eastern European origin. They were talking in their native language, deciding whether to buy a set of cups and saucers. The seller said, 'are you interested in purchasing this set today? They're hardly used. I bought them myself from the Crocker's a couple of years ago'. The couple looked indecisive, like they didn't want to make the purchase but after a few moments silence and consistent glaring from the seller, the couple the purchase. Perhaps this was a sign of complying with the community structures of the event in order to minimise the attention away from their ethnic identification, indeed an account of informal social control.

> (Field note taken from St. Peters craft fair, 1/11/13)

In conceptualising the control of difference through compliance of norms and values, Brickington's rural identity became something long-term residents actively protected, albeit through the tacit consumption of local goods (Giddens, 1993; Woodruffe-Burton, 1998). Featherstone (1992: 63) maintains that people create, sustain and protect whom they are through 'displaying their identity and sense of style in the particularity of the assemblage of goods, clothes, experiences and bodily dispositions they design together into a lifestyle'. To participate, therefore, in a rich symbolic rural environment, such as the craft fair and market, within which ruralised meanings were being attached to the objects being consumed, meant individuals outside of the dominant community of Brickington (e.g., those largely white, middle-class residents) had to either comply and buy into local life or be ostracised from the wider community by not participating. A similar analysis is discussed at length by Mort (1996: 137) in his account of the rise of *Burtons* amongst upper middle-class culture in 1950s Britain, whose techniques of salesmanship centred on protecting an affluent identity.

On the High Street

High streets fulfil many purposes. For many, they are more symbolic than just being a collection of shops. They are often a hub for the local community, providing a meeting place and offering a natural point for people to gather and socialise (Kendall, 2014). The look and feel of rural High Streets, in particularly, have dramatically changed over time. According to local archives, Brickington's High Street originally had just a cluster of shops; primarily local businesses ran by the local residents of the area. However, the town now plays host to an array of varied shops and shoppers:

> Walking into the town, I was immediately struck by its lack of the quaint rural feel that residents identified about the High Street. Having Costa Coffee next to a 'traditional', locally owned ornament shop gave a sense of heterogeneous, depicting heterotopic behaviour (cosmopolitan shopping habits vs. 'traditional' shopping habits) between long-term residents and newcomers, as well as urbanisation. I also noticed a Polish foods Shop that represented a sense of diversity on the High Street.

> (Field note taken from the High Street, 19/9/13)

The rise of the service industry and other changes on Brickington's High Street may have contributed to the growth of commuter shoppers; with more money to spend, shopping and dining in Brickington on the weekend became a great way for the affluent to buy into and consume a sense of rurality (Heley, 2008). This is evidenced by my direct observations conducted in Costa:

> A group of thirty-somethings talking about how they have come up from Waterloo train station to visit friends over the weekend and they are going back tomorrow. They are visiting Costa for

lunch. One mentions how he likes coming to Brickington every other weekend to do some shopping as it makes for a 'quieter shopping experience' and makes him feel likes he's in the country.

(Field note taken from Costa, 15/11/13)

However, chain stores such as Costa are not built out of a vacuum. The arrival of new businesses is contingent on supply and demand, and companies extend effort into researching the market to determine a shop's viability. Consequentially, the rise of the service industry in Brickington perhaps was not the consequence of the rise of commuter consumers but rather demand from those longer-term residents already in the town. This is demonstrated by my run in with Danielle in Costa:

> On the table in front of me I notice a familiar face looking around, waiting for her friend to come over with their cups of coffee. On noticing it was Danielle, I decided to go over to the table and say 'hi' and exchange casual pleasantries. She was very welcoming to see me and politely asked how the research was going. I responded by saying 'not bad…just sitting in cafes and walking around shops to see what local life in Brickington's all about'. After a couple of more exchanges of pleasantries I jokingly said 'what are you doing in Costa anyway?....I thought you hated its burnt taste and branded franchises'. She responded by shrugging my observation off and responded by saying 'Well…my friend wanted to come here. My ideal choice would be 811 Coffee, but we needed a caffeine boost and this was closest'.

(Field note taken from Costa, 15/11/13)

What the above field note demonstrates is that there is a clear difference between what long-term residents say they do and what long-term residents actually do. In other words, while long-term residents tended to buy into a discourse around the *idyllicisation* of rural life in Brickington within their conversations to me, including how they engaged in rural activities, or in Danielle's case how she only used or bought from local companies; in practice, their tacit actions were contributing to the changing nature of the High Street.

There was a perception amongst long-term residents that the ever-homogenizing feel and perhaps even gentrification of Brickington's High

Street had facilitated the diminution of Brickington's rural identity. However, from my own participant observations, the demolition, building upon and taking over of local businesses by chain stores appeared not to have eroded the town's sense of rural identity, specifically being enacted in everyday social interactions:

> Strolling through Brickington's High Street was an especially pleasurable episode during the fieldwork. It was an enlightening and informative experience about how locals created a sense of rurality in the town. Whilst walking through the town there was an obvious social capital between the people, I observed. This was noticeable in the passive interaction of two elderly men who walked past each other and said 'hello'.

> (Field note taken from the High Street, 4/10/13)

What is interesting from my direct observations along the High Street is that such passive social interactions tended to occur more often amongst older residents of the town. A plausible explanation for this is that those elderly residents I had observed were perhaps born and raised in the local area; therefore, going shopping on the High Street facilitated an idyllic perception of rural living in Brickington (e.g., a town of close-knit interaction) because the longer a person lives in their 'home' environment, the greater attachment to the area.

Such incidents of social interaction were not isolated cases; but rather, were often quite common throughout my time on the High Street. For instance, as I entered the locally famous Crocker's emporium, I saw Julie engaging in cheerful chatter with staff members, who later became known to me as David and John. The shop was a small affair, filled with bowls, plates, and other crockery utensils. On being noticed by Julie, she called me over and introduced me to David and John. After talking to David and John for some time, both Julie and I depart with the sound of laughter. 'I never leave Crocker's without a smile on my face. – all of the staff are so much fun – and you didn't even meet Steve, Peter or Tanya. When they're all together, it's like a comedy team!'

After disclosing to Julie, outside of the Crocker's emporium, I was conducting some research into local life on the High Street she insisted on showing me around some of the local businesses: 'I have to take you to one of my favourite shops in the town – Undercut's Clothing. There's a lovely lady called Hayley who runs it. You must go in!' I go in and meet Hayley who smiles sweetly and says, 'Welcome. How are you doing today sir?' The shop, itself, was a quaint experience. It was, like Crocker's emporium, a small shop, but despite its size, it was packed with social activity from (longer-standing?) residents shopping and engaged in chatter. There were also demonstrations of passive interactions taking place within this shop, with an elderly man sparking up a conversation with Hayley by simply saying 'morning'. 'I could stay here hours' Julie whispers to me. However, on this occasion, Julie does not. Back on the street and Julie points to some of the more ethnically diverse and franchised businesses, 'That's the Brickington Tandoori. It's one of the Indian restaurants that has opened up since the rise of chain stores and population growth. Most of its customers are mostly new residents that have moved in from London'.

A little further and we reach one of the local pubs – the Griffin – where Julie bought a round of coffee, while I took a seat. 'This is one of the oldest pubs in Brickington, and it's filled with locals' Julie enthuses as she tries to convince me that Brickington and its residents are typically rural. For a couple of minutes, my attention becomes fixated on three individuals dressed in Superman costumes who were collecting for a charity. Julie introduces me to these gentlemen, to who become known to me as Brendan, Neil, and Ken. 'Have you heard of Mulberry Court? It's a marvellous residential home for adults run by Scope and the Thorngrove Garden Centre that works with older people with disabilities. It has recently celebrated its 40th birthday', Brendan asks Julie. Julie responded by saying, 'Yes' and places a donation into the bucket. I reciprocated by doing the same, and then we finished our coffee and left.

What became clear during my participant observation and indeed guided tour of the Brickington High Street was Julie's constant performance of a Goffmanesque (1959) theatre. Within this context, Julie was presenting a 'best-suited narrative' of local life in Brickington. She was formally performing and adhering to the conventions that she thought represented the rural identity of Brickington, and as part of her dramaturgical performance she knew she was being watched and acted accordingly; consequentially, playing up to the audience that observed such constructions of rurality taking place (e.g., myself). Such performances included ignoring the wider social changes happening in Brickington – something which my own, independent participant observations on the High Street flagged up - by only fleetingly acknowledging the bigger or more diverse shops on the High Street and instead only showing me the local shops and pubs, which was rarely occupied by anybody other than longer-standing residents of the town.

In hindsight, I could have avoided Julie's dramaturgical performances of Brickington's rural identity by not disclosing my intention to observe the local life of the High Street. However, given that Julie was a resident who I had previously interviewed, I felt as though it was my ethical duty to be open and honest about my intentions while on the High Street. However, in doing so, I feel Julie's performance was an attempt on her part to demonstrate Brickington as being 'rural' to the observer.

Responsibilisation and rurality

The enactment of structural, ideological and cultural controls, through the routine activities of long-term residents, played a crucial role in the protection of Brickington's identity. This protection of Brickington identity, which seemed to centre on the construction and maintenance of rural identity and the presentation of the community as conforming with a specific set of norms relating to the ways in which long-term residents behaved, was of particular interest. Rose (2000) argues that social interaction and bonding can be the pathway through which local people focus their strategies for controlling social identity via responsibility and by establishing informal relations of specific individuals and particular populations (see also, Neal and Mooney, 2009), where for newcomers to belong they either have to accept 'unacceptance' or become socialised into the wider community.

Giddens' (1984) structuration theory would argue that such processes of informal social control occurred in Brickington because such routine activities were based on a person's position within a structured context that, in turn, enabled and restrained others' sense of belonging. We can see this playing out in the observational data cited above where the routines by particular residents to protect local identity were based on an unwitting attachment to the local landscape. This process is perhaps best further explained by Bobby who talked about the way 'traditional' form of buildings made residents interact:

> ....the historic buildings make local people share a common interest about the town. I mean...I was walking through the town centre the other day and got chatting to someone I know from the arts centre. We talked, just talked about how beautiful the buildings were there compared to elsewhere in the town; this common interest makes Brickington's sense of community stronger in a way.

This is also demonstrated by Kris in his interview when he describes how the local character of Brickington affects him emotionally:

> I love the town. I think there's a sense of togetherness in the town and all you need to do is to examine responses you get in the town to get a real feel of what people feel about Brickington. There is definitely a caring, sharing feel about this place. People

like me (and this is going to sound like bollocks!) but I have a high, celebrity-almost profile about the town; in the High Street, at the Rugby club people know me. So lots of people will speak to me. Nearly all of those though are old Brickington folk. For instance, I was out for a walk the other day and there was a guy walking towards me. He says "Hi Kris" and somewhere out of the back of my mind says "Hi Paul" and we chatted about Brickington and about the place. So it's this bond that has made the old Brickington folk closer and more close-knit, in a sense. Also, I think, in a way, this fondness I have about the town is because of how beautiful it looks. Granted you now have more urbanisation in Brickington; but the picturesque views of the fields and the red brick houses in the centre do, indeed, make me feel rural!

The way in which both Kris and Bobby move from the view of the local landscape to having strong social ties is imperative to note as it demonstrates the process through which people are seen as belonging in Brickington. When Kris, for example, emphasises that when he sees 'the fields' and the 'red brick houses in the centre' what gets gathered up and assigned are particular social, cultural and political meanings about the area, and it is these meanings which are facilitated by the interaction between local residents and the wider Brickington landscape. Words such as 'picturesque' in describing the scene of the historic town centre illustrate the disliking of the new housing areas of the town, and it is this subjective 'beauty' of the local architecture that makes residents feel a sense of attachment to the place.

Kris's use of expressions such as 'old Brickington folk' also implies the creation of social bonds which are exclusive to those who have longer-standing in Brickington. That is, they produced effective sites in which close-knit community interactions, such as those observed during my visits to *811 Coffee* and the St Peters craft fair and market and High Street, bound the social moods of long-term residents to the wider Brickington landscape. Thrift (2005), in his study of an urban community, talked about similar processes of these ever-present and ever busy but easily overlooked and 'forgotten infrastructure of social interaction' that routinely hold and bind people together and which are 'not easily unravelled' (Thrift, 2005: 136). According to Thrift (2005: 143), it is these everyday, routine interactions, which can provide the basis, through which towns and cities are able to invent and reinvent themselves. Viewing cities through such a lens reveals more about them being areas of control; where, not only are cities spaces in which diverse and exclusionary interactions are integral, but are also managed within them.

Social reproduction was an important element in the development of these social bonds (see the work of Gottfredson and Hirschi, 1990) in Brickington. Indeed, there was specific targeting of parents as key agents in enacting informal social control within the lives of their children, and an attempt to align their perspective towards one which conformed to the expected norms around Brickington's rural identity. Such process of responsibilisation can be seen in the way Susan talked about how passionate her two children were about the local community: 'my two children are hugely passionate about getting involved in the local community'. When questioned on what was it about Brickington that made her children actively involved in the community, Susan said:

> My family grew up in the town and so they are proud of it and feel part of it. My children want to grow up and feel safe and part of a community, not like it is becoming with the rise in chain stores and separated communities. So it is about being here for generations.

Hirschi (1969) would suggest that Susan's children's attachment to Brickington and their sense of community stemmed from a belief in the system of a particular rural identity that was socially reproduced on them by their parent(s). However, this process of responsibilisation is not always successful. In my interview with Helena and her son Ryan, Ryan who was born in Brickington but moved away to attend university in London expressed a lack of attachment to local life in Brickington:

> I'm in and out of Brickington a lot. I am currently studying Economics in London so I only really come back during study weeks. Because of my loss of connection to Brickington then I don't feel a connection anymore like I used to do.

According to Donnermeyer (2015), people's networks of belonging in rural areas are weakened when residents move out of the area and therefore break away from traditional values and customs of the local community. Thus for Ryan, his enjoyment of university - outings with friends and the hurried environment of London - became symbolic in the construction of his newly found identity and lifestyle and so was not keen to be involved in community life:

> I do enjoy going out with friends when I'm in London. We go out together after we've finished our classes and because of the fast-paced lifestyles of London I do not have time to think about everything, let alone feel a connection to the place. But, when I

come back here, it makes for a slower pace of life and people do feel a connection. I mean, I use to before I went to university. I see and hear people talk about the local community but I'm just not that bothered.

Ray and Reed (2005) argue that changes in lifestyle and preferred environment provide a space for which detachment from community social relations to form. In the case of Ryan, the fact that he chose to move away from Brickington and therefore detached himself from the ingrained values and traditions of the town meant that when he came back to the area the informal controls of social life, such as attachment to local customs and traditions, worked in such a way that separated him from the rest of the community, leaving behind only reminiscent tales of belonging.

The Neighbourhood Plan

So far in this chapter, I have discussed the social context that facilitated 'passive' processes of informal social control. Community social relations in Brickington created localised solidarities in micro-contextual environments, such as *811 Coffee*, St Peters craft fair and market and on the High Street, as an attempt ease long-term residents' 'existential anxieties' (Kinnvall, 2004) about change and globalisation by producing and reinforcing routines that gave rise to a sense of ontological security and insurance. In the following section, I will discuss accounts of 'active' processes of informal social control in which I will examine the use of the Neighbourhood Plan as an active community control used to protect Brickington's rural physical character.

A 'Neighbourhood Plan' is a way for local communities to decide the future of the place in which they live, introduced under the Localism Act (2010). The Localism Act (2010) provided communities with the direct power to develop a shared vision for their neighbourhood and deliver the sustainable development they need. According to the Brickington Neighbourhood Plan mission statement, its purpose is to provide 'guidelines for future development which is expressed to include a vision for the sort of place Brickington aims to be by 2026, together with an appropriate range of locally applicable development management policies. The latter would be formulated in such a way as to help further particular aspects of the vision of the plan'. This included the redevelopment of some areas of housing and the High Street in order to maintain a coherent theme and identity – that of the 'red brick' architecture seen in the centre of the town - running through the town. This would be achieved through cooperation between the Brickington Neighbourhood Planning Group (BNPG) and the local council by way of policies that make provisions for future changes to the centre and surrounding areas of Brickington; and also, by rejuvenating community life through hosting local events which reflect the traditional customs and values of the town.

The southern extension

The Neighbourhood Plan was a response by some of the residents over the planned southern extension. The southern extension was a housing development project that involved building 1500 new houses in the surrounding green space of Brickington along its southern end (The Commons area). The proposed plans by the council had made some residents angry. Jane's anger was directed at the unsustainability of the new development and the unsympathetic housing designs the extension would bring:

> The planned southern extension is the main concern for us in the town. The local council are planning to extend housing into the field located behind (local garden centre) in the south of the town. Apparently there are going to be 1500 new homes being built and it makes me so cross! Brickington can't sustain anymore building. The recent buildings dotted around the town are already a mess and they're planning to build more; we're going to lose our uniqueness as a town!

Whilst Julie's anger was targeted at the loss of local identity:

> We're going to lose our identity. You've got neighbouring villages which are perfect villages you'd see on a packet of fudge but Brickington itself is a mess. The local council are planning to extend along the southern route in and out of the town, building blocks of flats and housing estates which are going to be completely out of character.

Deborah agreed with Julie by mentioning the harmful impact such a top-down approach of planning would have on the identity of Brickington:

> I think it's detrimental to our rural community. The council are deciding for us how and what type of houses are being built we are losing our individuality – the traditional red brick houses in the centre come to mind.

Erosion of local character

These residents' fears of the southern expansion seemed to be built around the impact the development would have on the local character of the area.

Current housing developments have tended to create a dichotomy between the different housing styles in Brickington: 'traditional' housing styles – e.g., 'red brick' or coarse rubble architecture - in the centre and non-traditional housing styles – e.g., reconstructed stone or brown brick architecture - around the peripheral. The concerns long-term residents had pertained to the homogenisation of place these non-traditional styles would bring, which tend to be based on modern standards of design rather than being unique to the town. Such concerns can be heard in the comments made by Joseph:

> ...Brickington housing has grown like wild fire....Whereas, before we had a few scattered council houses, we have now got several estates holding residents that have moved into Brickington, and it's chaos. I mean each road on these estates lead onto one another; and the houses look run down. And the local residents are up in arms about it.

The housing styles on the Fields estate, located in the Marsh area of town, consisting of late-20th Century designs best illustrates Joseph's point. These houses tended to be more about the national standard design and materials of the developer rather than being in sympathy with the local character of Brickington. Instead of being built out of coarse rubble or red brick, newer builds utilised variation through a mixture of brick colours in simple banding details, such as Cherryfields (see Figure 6.1 – picture on top), or had a relatively random mixture of bricks and rendered walls, together with slate and concrete tiled roofs such as the estate designs in the Commons area of Brickington (see Figure 6.1 – picture on bottom).

Principally then, the look and feel about Brickington's architecture that some residents latched onto (see Chapter 5) as representing a particular local identity is seen as being relatively eroded through insensitive design. These anxieties that some residents felt about the lack of identity were often targeted towards the developers who often bring with them their own way of developing houses; and so, they get applied wherever the developer builds. This targeted resentment towards developers was made very explicit by Melissa:

> ...The property developers are saying they want to create something that is a bit exciting and not just rows of boring houses. In terms of actual building, you've got mixed building designs all over Brickington, all of which aren't in-keeping with the traditional design of the town, and the aesthetic. They're looking at the houses and all of the aesthetics and saying "we don't want similar houses. We want unique and individualistic houses". But that isn't what the countryside is about. We want red brick and

traditional stone houses which are free-flowing and beautiful; rural!!

Figure 6.1 – Non-traditional Housing Types

Photos taken from Brickington Neighbourhood Plan (2012)

However, it is important to note that the buildings that are fondly looked on as being 'traditional Brickington' now were most likely developers' idealisation according to market demand when they were built. Therefore reiterating the idea that what gets used to form Brickington identity is largely based on some residents' 'imaginings' of the local area; which, over time have become structurally ingrained into the local area that it becomes symbolic of their particular rural identity.

Spatial power

What appears to be implicit in the discussions above about concerns of erosion of local character is the use of the Neighbourhood Plan as a form of power. The Neighbourhood Plan is being used by long-term residents as a certain type of power: a type of power Massey (1994) calls 'spatial power' - the ability of residents to take control or resist, against unwanted social change. This was evidenced in the way Melissa spoke about the purpose of the 'Neighbourhood Plan':

> ...the Neighbourhood Plan is acting as protection against these developments and migration into the town from spiralling out of control. One aspect of the Neighbourhood Plan is to allow lifetime residents and people who have been here fifteen, twenty years to have a say on where housing can be built, what form this can take and who or what is representative of Brickington. Myself, personally, I am working closely with planners to identify where and what they can build.

The Neighbourhood Plan, therefore, can be seen as a sort of boundarised refuge in which local residents are able to feel in control of change, as was further articulated by Melissa:

> There is an element of a "we need to protect our rural heritage type of thing" attitude in the local plan. We've had a visit from National Trust and English Heritage talking about the dangers of urban sprawl and not protecting our rurality, if you like and I think that is very much a feature of the plan...So there's a protectionist element to it. That the clansmen, kingship, that sorta thing; where anything outside of the rural way of life is treated with suspicion and difference.

Rural heritage had a direct impact on the way residents talked about Brickington. 'The rural landscape of Brickington is very much part of our heritage' Barbara said positively:

> We have the beauty of the English countryside on our doorstep and I love looking at it. It's also very peaceful. We're surrounded by fields. You've only got to go a few yards and you'll be in one.

> Even with the building that have gone on since we first arrived here, which has expanded, but we still only have to go a very little way and you'll be in a field. I know it's romantic and all the rest of it, and the traditional way of life will never really come back, but I think it's what a lot of people, certainly the lifelong residents of the town, crave. You know, we like things the way they used to be and I think we're going to get there, eventually, with the local plan.

What this quotation is implying is that certain residents – especially those of middle-class background and longer-standing in the town – are looking back to what was, the past, to protect against the uncertainty of the future. This can be seen in Joseph's description of the influence of topography in establishing a particular image that reflects the rural nature of Brickington:

> I do consider Brickington a rural town. You're surrounded by countryside. Surrounded by all those fields and hills and trees and rivers and all of that sorta stuff. We also have these pocket communities interacting with each other and you do see people randomly bump into someone and start a conversation.

This 'fixing' of rural heritage through the 'Neighbourhood Plan' reinforced what Lash and Urry (1994: 211) concede as the commodification of place involving an 'increased sensitivity to local features...and place myths'. 'Place-myths' are important as they describe socio-cultural understanding and establish particular identities by registering fear/threat of and need to resist change by, what Sibley (1997: 78) calls, 'the erection of strong boundaries'; or to put it simply, the constructed symbolic boundaries regarding the way people talk about their area. In this context, the Neighbourhood Plan was used by a particular group of residents who had vested interests in emphasising and reconfirming the 'place-myths' (Scott and Hogg, 2015: 36); or, all the things that makeup, form and from which is supposed to be representative of Brickington identity. Below I want to spend some time examining the ways in which longer-term residents attempt to control the 'place-myths' of Brickington identity.

Bringing back the 'chocolate box'

The use of spatial power to protect the physical form of the built environment can reinforce protectionist feelings in residents of communities (Steventon, 2001; Suttles, 1972). Suttles (1972), for example, maintains that residents cognitively attach meaning to certain physical aspects of their locality to discretely define boundaries that demarcate their distinction from other groups. The desire to reclaim and redevelop buildings into 'traditional' forms, as expressed in the Neighbourhood Plan, therefore acts as a set of discursive symbols that gets used to define the rural nature of Brickington and exercise power to protect local identity. A similar analysis can be heard in the seminal work of Matless (1994), where he acknowledges the discursive representations of 'traditional' architecture is defended out of preservationist nostalgia, while also dismissed as a requirement to modernise the countryside and to seek new ways of protecting local identity.

The extracts below evidence this in the way local talk about particular buildings and features of the local built environment being representative of Brickington identity were fed into discourse around local change and therefore a need for the Neighbourhood Plan:

> *Steven:* ...the Town Planning Team has spent three years putting together a town design statement defining what really needs to happen here. I think the problem with Brickington over the last few years is that there hasn't been a lot of thought about how much Brickington has changed and the impact housing has had upon it. Because of this the design of Brickington is mismatch. You've got some of the modern buildings, such as Kingfisher Avenue and the Fields which look dreadful. We need more of the traditional buildings, like the really nice stuff in Brickington - the church in the centre and the Brickington red brick buildings – they really show off our identity as a town.

> *Jane:* People do generally prefer these independent retailers and this is because they offer quirkiness and chocolate-box style shops rather than these big chains such as Asda who tend to be solely focused on profit and based in a giant tin building!. The town team are attempting to bring this style of High Street back, but it will take a while.

What these remarks cited above imply is the Neighbourhood Plan's ability to work as a 'refuge from late-modernity' (Short, 1992: 34). It becomes used as a strategy for resisting globalised social change, such as urbanisation and neoliberalism, by rekindling the past (Tucan, 1980; Olwig, 1982) and enabling residents to develop a sense of place and ontological security.

Conclusion

The central theme running through this chapter has been the desire to protect Brickington's rural identity from wider issues of social change. Long-term residents' expression for a shared rural identity, which incorporated the values they held and the way the local landscape was represented, facilitated the enactment of informal social control. This enactment of informal social control took two forms: 'passive' structural, ideological and cultural controls, and 'active' community controls. The data demonstrated that by long-term residents presenting themselves as 'rural' in public settings such as *811 Coffee*, St. Peters craft fair and market and within the High Street, they enacted passive controls as a response to the impact of social change and globalisation on the identity of the place. Likewise, this chapter also illustrated how resistance to change also took an 'active' form. This was made evident through an examination of the Brickington Neighbourhood Plan: a community-led plan challenging social change.

What is evident from the data cited throughout this chapter is the ways in which informal social control was seen to operate within Brickington. Some of the long-term residents who I interviewed yearned for a return to traditional rural life in Brickington in order to combat the negative consequences of change. This was often mirrored by their own experiences of growing up in a community where 'everyone knew everyone' and where a sense of community was felt much more strongly across Brickington. For long-term residents, the idea of harping back to past ideals of rural community relations, therefore, played a crucial role in not only the operation of informal social control but also the facilitation of their own very traditional ideas of what rural life in Brickington should be like.

Moreover, in enacting informal social control, long-term residents also called on their own empowerment that was co-constitutively given to them by the government under the Localism Act (2010). What the data in this chapter has further demonstrated, therefore, is that increased localism enabled residents with greatest emotional and psychological investment in local life to take action against processes of social change that perilously threatened the rural identity of the town. However, while the enactment of informal social control by long-term residents in Brickington was based around rhetoric and discourse of social change, such processes of control also had the unintended consequences of controlling difference and diversification. This complicated the enactment of informal social control in Brickington as such efforts to resist change resulted in unintentional exclusionary and indeed racist consequences in order to protect Brickington's rural identity. This is what the next chapter now turns to.

Chapter 7

'Where are you from and what are you doing here?': Exclusionary consequences of informal social control

Introduction

In Chapter 6 I denoted the routine activities and actions some long-term residents used to resist and control Brickington's specific rural identity and character. Chapter 6 demonstrated that the enactment of informal social control sought to protect the rural identity of Brickington in two ways. 'Passive' everyday routines enacted in public places such as *811: Coffee*, the St. Peters craft fair and market and along the High Street sought to protect the ideological, structural and cultural controls of Brickington rural identity, while community controls were used to 'actively' resist against the changing rural character of the town. However, despite some long-term residents working up such routines and actions as a means to protect the town's identity against the perceived erosion of its rural identity and character, this discourse was - by and large - a smokescreen for fear of newcomers.

In the following chapter, therefore, I want to explore the exclusionary consequences of informal social control. The first part of this chapter will do this by arguing that the enactment of informal social control manifested from a broader concern of newcomers. I suggest here that long-term residents' concerns about social change were less attributable to fears of the erosion of rural identity and character, but more to the structural processes of resisting newcomers which had an unanticipated consequence of creating an exclusive and exclusionary rural community.

The second part of this chapter goes on to detail the experiences/feelings of racism expressed by some minority ethnic residents in Brickington. In this, I argue that while all newcomers were excluded from local life in Brickington, minority ethnic residents were doubly excluded based on their perceived differences being more readily atypical of the town's specific rural identity.

Through the unpacking of minority ethnic residents experiences, this chapter highlights racism as an unanticipated consequence of informal social control that sought to protect and maintain the specific rural identity of the town.

Wider concern of newcomers

Cloke (1992) argues that protectionist narratives - such as those discussed in Chapter 6 - have been used by rural dwellers to normalise a particularly anti-outsider ethos (see also, Newby, 1979; Murdoch, 2003). This can be seen in Brickington where the actions used by long-term residents in developing the 'Neighbourhood Plan' can be interpreted as having deeper symbolic significance. For instance, the 'Neighbourhood Plan' can be interpreted as a smokescreen for, and also give rise to, a sense of wariness about newcomers and who social change may bring into Brickington. Such concerns can be read in Joseph's remark below:

> You see the council are planning to expand (the Commons) by building new housing estates. But if people started seeing these estates popping up to accommodate a few newcomers what you'd see is agro amongst locals about the effects it would have on the town.

The following extracts taken from interviews with Danielle and Marc also support this analysis:

> *Danielle:* It has changed, definitely. It's much, much more diverse now. Brickington has always been white but with ongoing developments in the town, people have moved in and settled here and you can see this at the local primary school. The younger years are starting to fill up with a much bigger mix, for example the Polish and that's causing a bit of trouble.

> *Marc:* I've noticed little things like replacing a field with a river running it with a car park for the local Waitrose. And that's kind of problematic, I mean it takes away that pretty Brickington feeling...you know...that we use to have. We now have new communities in the area, particular from Eastern European...Brickington does have a large(ish) Polish community.

Those who I had spoken to were remarkably guarded about their feelings concerning newcomers, but the generalised anxiety that newcomers in Brickington were greeted crept into the many conversations I had with long-term residents. A common view among these residents was that the town was close-knit and therefore unwittingly apprehensive of those perceived to be newcomers. Steven, for example, stated that despite welcoming newcomers into the town they are often 'scrutinised' by long-term residents due to an 'inevitable legacy of traditional rural-urban cultural divides' (Chakraborti, 2007: 125) where long-term residents tended only to associate with other long-term residents: 'I'd welcome anyone into Brickington, but there is always a suspicion about new people at first. Even the people who have come from London!' This can also be seen in the quotation below taken from my conversation with Deborah:

> Generally people, particularly those with historical connections don't like other people coming in. This has nothing to do with racism, or whatever, we'd welcome anybody regardless. There is just a general suspicion of people from outside Brickington.

Deborah's remark is interesting here as it suggests a naturalisation of residents' fear/threat of newcomers. Her use of the phrase 'generally people, particularly those with historical connections' indicates that the feelings of distrust towards newcomers is greater amongst those who have been born and bred in the area and have seen the town change over time. Giddens' (1984: 282) structuration theory would argue that this happens because people position themselves as a way to ensure legitimacy and domination to a particular identity - he refers to these as 'position-practices' – which has the ability to structure the position of the individual in relation to that of others.

This process of positioning became clear as the interviews went on as newcomers were categorised. For those residents who have lived in Brickington for generations, anyone raised outside of the Brickington community was seen as an outsider. However, some residents (including those who were initially seen as newcomers but now had some local standing) used the term 'newcomer' as a device to define newer residents. For instance, both Margaret and Steven talked about how their fear of the erosion of local rural identity had palpably increased since the arrival of the Polish:

> *Margaret*: I shouldn't be saying this because it is discriminatory and I could be seen as a racist. But I am wary of the Polish people that have moved into Brickington. I am very dubious about what they're doing here. It is getting harder and harder to tell who's Polish and who's not.
>
> *Steven*: There is a large percentage of Polish in the town. They work locally in the factories. This has occurred in the last six to

seven years….It has made me more suspicious of newcomers, because of the Polish. And it's not just Polish, it's Polish, Latvians and Czechoslovakians and all the rest of them that moved here. It could affect the social cohesion of the community if more and more of these people continue to come in and what is left of our slice of the English countryside will be gone.

What is being suggested here is that there is a shared consciousness amongst long-term residents in Brickington that minority ethnic individuals do not form part of Brickington identity and that there are feelings of distrust towards them, particularly amongst the more well-established residents of the town. However, the interviews revealed a corpus of prejudices about the Polish residents that seemed to be based on myth and stereotype, as the following comments from Margaret indicate:

> There is a lot of Polish now that live in Brickington. But, in my opinion, and I hate to say this because I might be seen as a terrible thing. I don't like it. Not because of who they are, the Polish fought for us in the war, but because Brickington when I first arrived here was a small, hard-working English country town but with the Polish here it's changed. They're not hard-working, they're lazy.

These kinds of generalised statements were regularly expressed by a particular group of residents, mainly white, middle-class with longer-standing in the town, during conversations about newcomers. Connolly (2006) maintains that the distrust rural communities have towards newcomers is based on their portrayal in the British media as being atypical within countryside spaces. In other words, distrust of newcomers is largely contingent on what people have heard or read about in the local and national news rather than their own lived experiences of it. Consequently then, the types of opinions which long-term residents expressed towards the Polish in Brickington was not surprising. Like Traveller communities in Chakraborti's (2007) research that had experienced feelings of exclusion about how they were perceived by the local community, whose opinions were based on the media's perception of them more than anything else, the Polish residents in Brickington experienced a similar feeling - something which was acknowledged by Jerzy and Rafael:

> *Jerzy*: The people of the town think that we are here to do them over and steal their jobs and because there has been an increase of us that we're making opportunities for these new businesses, such as Costa to come in

> *Rafael:* There is a lot of scaremongering going around that we're here to take jobs, or that we're lazy.

Interestingly, although residents' comments about the Polish residents were – by and large – negative, long-term residents did seem to acknowledge Polish residents as less of a 'direct threat'. Instead, people's observations of the Polish in Brickington tended to centre on the broader impact of Polish and wider Eastern European immigration that was happening in Britain: as these quotations from Steven and Marc highlight:

> *Steven:* ...I don't think it makes so much difference as far as, erm – as far as Brickington is concerned; Brickington is always going to be Brickington. But the Polish, people from the Eastern Bloc countries, you know, they've been gradually moving to England and so it is going to have an impact nationally.

> *Marc:* I think that was something changed a national level than a local one. Perhaps Brickington is a bit further behind. I mean we've got Polish communities....some residents – mainly the old folks – turn their nose up but, that is just the way the countryside is.

The data here resonates with the literature highlighted in Chapter 3 that seemed to suggest that the population of rural towns and villages are vastly expanding, ergo creating tensions between different groups in local communities. This also accompanies suggestions by Hubbard (2006) who articulated in his research on the resistance to asylum seekers in the south of England that the higher the levels of anti-asylum rhetoric and discourse, the more the rural community is attempting to distance themselves (socially and geographically) from the multiculturalism and diversity of the city.

However, whilst there were some, perhaps unwittingly negative, opinions expressed towards the Polish, longer-term residents seemed to accept professional and generally more affluent newcomers as they appeared to be more representational of the conventional norms, values, and beliefs of Brickington. This is observable in the interviews I conducted with affluent newcomers:

> *Irvin:* Most people from well-off or professional backgrounds: you, know, people who've got the money, can buy the houses, that sort of thing. They're accepted because they are respected and revered.

> *Barbara*: People who are well-educated professionals, they're not perceived as outsiders or anything like that. They're really part of the community. I think because of my position, as a local magistrate, and as someone who came from a very upper middle-class background, local people sort of accepted me into the community.

What the data is illustrating is that boundaries of acceptance are not fixed. They vary and are contingent on the perceived class status or occupation of the newcomer. In particular, doctors were marked as being 'acceptable' newcomers, although tellingly it seemed as though this acceptance was contingent on their ability to position themselves with the values and norms of Brickington. This was something that was especially evident in my interview with Julie as she talked about a local doctor of Ethiopian descent: 'We do have a doctor who is from Ethiopia; he's dark but very posh. He makes a wonderful contribution to the community: helps out at local events, very approachable, that sort of thing'.

Therefore, it appeared that as long as newcomers could position, or align themselves with Brickington identity, then they might be accepted or approved of within the community. And, of course, being identified as having a signifier of perceived social status can be useful for those minority ethnic individuals who might otherwise be seen in a similar light as the Polish residents referred to above. Nevertheless, the assimilation of middle-class values and customs to ascertain 'cultural capital' for newcomers within rural communities can only get minority ethnic individuals so far. Ultimately though, rural communities have specific sets of cultural sensibilities and practical knowledges which determine the extent to which minority ethnic individuals are able to fit into the social networks of rural community life (Tyler, 2006), leading to the realisation that no matter how much newcomers attempt to fit in, true insider status is rarely given (Sibley, 1997).

An exclusive rural community

What is drawn out and demonstrated in the data cited above is a rhetoric of an anxious community – marked by the explicit symbolism of boundaries; of discourses around insiders and outsiders; of external threat and internal danger. The Neighbourhood Plan and indeed Julie's actions on the High Street (as discussed in Chapter 6) can be seen as a type of Goffmanesque (1999 – originally published in 1956) theatre – a management and public demonstration of the 'best narrative' of Brickington life. This is not to say that such best narratives did not exist in Brickington but rather to suggest that the local routines and actions of residents tend to create them (see also, Neal and Walters, 2006).

Such desires to recreate this best-suited narrative of what Brickington life is supposed to be like, however, tended to produce a rural community that was exclusive and excluding. The notion of rural community and its reproduction of exclusivity was something that also troubled Rees (1950).

The interviews and discussions with some long-term residents of Brickington gave rise to themes of 'the powerful and emotive' concept of local rural community (Francis and Henderson, 1992: 19). Those interviewed maintained that Brickington was both welcoming to newcomers and yet also 'close-knit', highlighting that everyone knew everybody else. Look at the following extracts for example:

> *Jane:* Brickington is a small rural town. Everybody knows each other and it is very close-knit. Everybody's really friendly and even new people say how warm they were welcomed and, as I say, people go in the council office, you know and ask about council tax and bin days and so on and they say how warmly they were welcomed in the town.

> *Steven:* ...as I say, the town's very close-knit. I do think it's changed a bit. You can walk up through the High Street and know everybody you pass. You know, you can go into the surgery and start talking to anybody in the waiting room. Even the newer residents feel welcomed. I have a Polish girl staying with me, a lodger, she says how nice everybody is.

What these extracts depict is the importance of markers of local life in Brickington — familial ties, length of residency and conviviality — and these are reflected in Abrams' (2003: 82) study where residents she talked to saw their village 'as a timeless place of long-established families forming a stable core of "real community"'. Rural identity, therefore, in the eyes of long-term residents has an "ageless' quality, as though rural areas are "frozen' in time and located in a mythologised, perhaps even pre-war, era of stability and tranquillity' (Neal and Agyeman, 2006a: 175). However, as Abram (2003: 82) observes, there is a contradiction to this idyllicised myth of the countryside in which the long-term residents she had talked to were disgruntled by the arrival of new residents as a result of housing development, with one stating: 'Everybody in the queue in front of you at the fête is [now] a stranger. It's rather as if you've moved'. This is reflected in the conversations I had with Steven and Danielle where, despite proclaiming Brickington was a welcoming town, they often felt threatened:

Steven: ...I would definitely say it's changed. I mean when I lived here as a child there were only 2,500 residents and the community atmosphere. But, because of supermarket chains and new housing developments, to me and other residents, it's lost its rural charm and productivity. There's no local cattle markets or anything like that anymore. Most of the farmers round 'ere find it hard to make any sort of profit. What this change in the town has done is brought in families, and I don't want to seem offensive, from different cultural backgrounds and I think this has downgraded the rural feel of the town.

Danielle: Brickington has changed and it has changed massively. Brickington was a lot different when I was growing up. Everybody knew everybody and so everybody knew who I was and so I couldn't do anything without being taken back to my parents. So from that aspect it's changed; you can't really get to know everybody anymore as you used to. The population has doubled and there are a lot more new residents than there was when I was young.

This fear of difference reflects a view of Brickington that closely resemble Bauman's (2001: 15) notion of 'afraid and anxious individuals', where the insecurities and fears of imagined external threats among long-term residents have resulted in a 'drawbridge' mentality which is systematically and institutionally suspicious of newcomers. The findings, therefore, suggest that while long-term residents' concerns about newcomers moving in and disrupting local life may be 'imagined', the changes happening in the town were a reality and so were collectively shared amongst those residents with a greater sense of attachment to Brickington identity. Thus, this fearful mentality about newcomers formed what Bauman (2001: 15) calls a 'peg community': 'an imagined community identity that offers collective insurance against individually confronted uncertainties'. The construction of such communities may not be discursively known, but their existence is rooted in the practical knowledge of long-term residents who are tacitly aware that others share the same concerns and feel the same about safeguarding their way of life.

Some of the residents I interviewed noted how their Brickington identity had become increasingly threatened due to these processes of globalisation. Kris, in particularly, highlighted:

we are getting to look more and more like everywhere else it is important to bring into community life individualism; a real, strong sense of rural identity...change has affected everything.

> And what I think we, and I say we in a very broad sense, would prefer is, erm, a feeling of identity, reflected by these traditional rural values.

It makes sense, in this context, to see the process of social change work in an iterative and recursive way in Brickington, where the need for identity to maintain ontological certainty is brought about because of the marking out of difference. Bobby offers an explanation about how Brickington identity is used to maintain ontological certainty: 'the more change that happens in Brickington, the more we need to cling onto this idea of Brickingtonness, and this sense of Brickingtonness is reflected in everything we do'.

What Bobby is alluding to here is that as social change happens some residents are effectively conjuring up Brickington identity as something which is precarious and perilously threatened: and as Wright (2008: 312) states, 'even in peacetime, the countryside can feel like a perpetual Dunkirk, in which everything that is valued is polarised against encroaching developments that promise only nullification and destruction'. Thus, it is through this perceived 'nullification' and 'destruction' of Brickington's local character and way of life that long-term residents used routines and action in order to maintain ontological security; and it was the enactment of such informal social control that often worked in exclusive and excluding ways.

Experiences of racism

It became clear during the interviews that the process of social exclusion in Brickington was equally applicable to any newcomer: a point Bobby makes when recalling his efforts to integrate into the local community when he first moved to Brickington, which tended to include visiting one of the local pubs – *The Griffin*:

> *Bobby:* When I first moved here I thought it'd be a great opportunity to meet some of the locals by going down to the pub. However, when you stepped in they'd make it clear I was not allowed. I remember ordering a pint and trying to talk to some of the locals but they'd just ignored me.

However, experiences of social exclusion were worse for minority ethnic newcomers on the grounds of their obvious differences that separated them from the norms of Brickington, and because social exclusion operated more ardently against minority ethnic individuals, such exclusionary processes can be seen as racist processes respectively. Those minority ethnic residents I interviewed spoke negatively about their lived realities in Brickington and their social bonds with other residents in the town. However, not all accounts were overly negative; in fact, some minority ethnic individuals mentioned, albeit partially, being included in certain contexts. In highlighting such dynamic process, therefore, I want to unpack and analyse some of the experiences of racism articulated by some of the minority ethnic residents to bring light to the complexity of the boundaries asserted by Brickington identity.

"Where are you from and what are you doing here?"

One theme that came out of the research was that some minority ethnic residents often felt excluded because longer-standing residents would act differently towards them, as their appearance was something that many residents were not familiar with. This is best captured by Faseeh in the following way:

> Sometimes you get a sense that the don't want you here but I don't think it's that they're being racist or anything like that it is simply because I am of a darker skin colour and that is very out of place in Brickington. Once I called and made an appointment at the bank, I said "Hi, my name is Faseeh and I am from Mauritius". Now, I shouldn't really have to say that but I've noticed that when I don't people will say "Where you from and what you doing here?" and it feels very isolating knowing that people perceive my ethnicity.

This fascination with the exoticism of those minority ethnic residents who look and sound different from the 'norms' of rural life has, what some researchers (e.g., Plastow, 2011; Neal, 2009; Neal and Agyeman, 2006a and 2006b; Chakraborti and Garland, 2006) have argued, contributed to the negative experiences of rural living for minority ethnic individuals. For example, in Robinson and Gardner's (2006: 45) study, some minority ethnic residents felt their 'exoticism' had an impact on achieving a sense of belonging and was often cited as a detrimental factor in choosing not to move into rural communities. This understanding of minority ethnic individuals in rural contexts as being 'exotic' was reflected by Jay (1992: 21) in his study of South-west England where he records the life-experiences of a Black resident:

> For one man, the experience of being a black person in an almost totally white environment was that he encouraged and was regarded as a piece of 'exotica'…They treated me as someone who needed to be patronised; it was as though I had just stepped off the boat.

In the context of my study, Marie felt especially uneased having the authenticity of her ethnic difference being actively challenged during the course of day-to-day life:

> When I go up to pay at the market and they hear my accent they will ask "Where are you from" and "What made you come and live here"? It's very off-putting; it makes me feel different, like of I'm some sort of novelty.

This account of actively challenging of ethnic difference, which crept into my interviews with minority ethnic residents, is supported by the direct observational data. During my direct observations in *Couch Potato*, one of the local cafes adjacent to the High Street, I noticed a Black woman come in and order a sandwich and cup of tea. On observing what I thought to be a mundane occurrence, I overheard the conversation of two elderly (long-term?) white residents in which one turned to the other and said, *"There's a black woman in Brickington".* It is these more subtle, but equally insidious, forms of racisms that operated out longer-standing residents' surveillance of difference that made minority ethnic residents in my study feel isolated and excluded. Faseeh, for instance, stated that being one of the very few visibly black people in Brickington made him feel like 'the odd one out' because he was not white.

A similar conclusion was drawn by Malcolm (2004: 71) who noted how obtrusive staring was a common factor in the exclusionary forms of harassment some minority ethnic residents felt in his study. Two Asian women Malcolm spoke to articulated how they were regularly stared at by staff in restaurants and often it was not until they explicitly asked for them to stop they would.

Despite this process of racism happening, Faseeh did state that his visible and cultural difference did not cause him any problems:

> I spend a lot of my time working, and working in Yeovil as well so my interaction with the area is quite fragmented. I don't really know where certain places are in the town and even people ask me about where I'm from I take it as a question of interest because I am not really known in Brickington, and not about my race.

Chakraborti's (2007) study in rural Warwickshire provides similar arguments in which minority ethnic individuals working away in more multicultural environments of Coventry, Nuneaton and Leicester had helped to understand long-term residents' inquisitiveness in the more remote rural areas of the county.

"I had to hide behind my husband's identity"

Another theme that emerged out of the data on racism was the fact that minority ethnic individuals felt the need to, almost unwittingly, guard against the gaze of the Brickington community by suppressing their own identities. This is best seen by Ann who talked about the way she had to hide her Colombian heritage behind her husband's Welsh identity in order to fit in.

> I do feel as though I am an outsider because the local residents of Brickington would see you and stare and I say "Where you come from!!" and I thought if I was truly part of the town I wouldn't have been asked where I came from they would just accept it. My husband is Welsh and so I had to hide behind my husband's identity. It got to a point where when people asked me where I came from I'd reply "I'm Welsh" and I thought in this way I would appear less alien than if I said I am Colombian.

A similar account of 'fitting in' is highlighted by Derbyshire (1994: 33) in her study of a Norfolk village where she demonstrated how the onus is always on minority ethnic residents to fit into rural society, and in her interviews with minority ethnic groups illustrate how coping with life in rural society requires compromise and self-denial.

What the data is suggesting is that even when minority ethnic people are content to strive for acceptance from the wider Brickington community, they face an inevitability that acceptance will usually only be partial. This was the case with Ann in which despite feeling uncomfortable and often excluded from life in Brickington, she also expressed feelings of acceptance whilst talking about her involvement in church activities. She expressed how long-term residents made her feel welcome when she made efforts to join in with locally based social activities hosted by the local Church:

> It's still 'Them and I" and I don't think that'll ever disappear. And I think this is because of my Colombian background living in the English countryside. The church helped me a lot to integrate into life in Brickington. Because in the church it was the only place I felt equal to the others. When I'm in the church they accept me and I am equal to them.

Therefore, to a certain extent, Ann's acceptance into Brickington life was only partial, and this was largely contingent on her ability to suppress her Colombian identity – which did not fit the norms of the town – in favour of her Christian identity that long-term residents perceived to be more in-touch with the character of local life. As Ann explained:

> In the church, I am seen as being equal. I am Christian and accepted rather than Colombian and different. And because of this most people don't see me as Colombian, I am mainly considered to be part of the Christian community here in Brickington.

This conditional acceptance into rural life can be seen in Esuantsiwa-Goldsmith and Makris's (1994: 22) study where an Asian women interviewee maintained:

> The attitude of white society in rural areas appears contradictory. They imply that if minority people conform and adopt white culture they will be accepted. But even if we do we are still regarded as different.

Similarly, the research of Tyler (2006) articulates that the 'rural village' acts as a stage which both enables and restrains people's ties to the community. Drawing on interviews with middle-class residents from Greenville, a village suburb of Leicester, Tyler explored the way in which residents protected and maintained their area's rural identity through a rhetoric of 'othering' that ostracised Asian individuals. Tyler (2006: 396) found that, although Asian residents had 'achieved economic parity with the more affluent wealthy white middle-class residents, local residents thought they lacked the 'proper' middle-class values of respectability and decorum, which are associated with the traditional white rhythms of English village life'; thus, restraining their entitlement to the area.

This pressure for minority ethnic residents to take on board Brickington identity in order to become indistinguishable from the rest of the town is clearly noted in the wider literature on rural exclusion (e.g., Jay, 1992; de Lima, 2001; Chakraborti, 2007). The existence of exclusive insider positions within Brickington, unwittingly, allowed long-term residents to determine who does and who does not belong; consequentially, leading to a system which served to reinforce long-term residents sense of identity by reemphasising their place within Brickington, whilst diminishing the claims to Brickington identity by minority ethnic residents.

Little Poland

Another example of racism was the case of the Polish food shop on the High Street called *Little Poland* and owned by Kara. Kara pointed out that 'the shop did really well in its first year in Brickington…(which) had a big Polish community, so I had tonnes of customers coming in and wanting to buy groceries. Several people became regulars, and I became very familiar with them. I enjoyed it'. Kara's relative success of running *Little Poland* as an ethnic food store on the High Street had to do with the extensive list of Polish residents who shopped there. The relationships between Kara and her 'regulars' became close because of their shared culture as well as diet and culinary preferences. This point was made explicitly clear by Kara who articulated:

> Little Poland was a hub for the Polish residents in the town. It became a place where we felt like ourselves. We could speak in Polish and do things our own way without the worry of people questioning us.

The feelings of exclusion experienced by Kara and possibly her customers, however, provided a sense of solidarity. This manifested itself in subtle ways such as having a shared diet, and as a result, made Little Poland a social space for Polish residents with a shared ethnic background to meet and socialise. Before long, however, such collective expressions of solidarity based upon shared cultural and culinary practices expressed by Kara diminished quickly when her 'regulars' decided to leave Brickington and return to Poland as a result of the declining British economy and the rising Polish economy: 'After eighteen months most of my "regulars" decided to leave Brickington and go back to Poland'. Consequentially, Little Poland stopped attracting customers, as long-term residents did not need to shop there. This is seen in Melissa's account when asked why she does not shop in Little Poland:

> I don't go into Little Poland because it sells nothing I need. I don't oppose places like that on the High Street; it is fine by me if it stays there. I just will never need to use it.

Similarly, Steven said:

> I don't have a problem with it being there. I've never been inside Little Poland, as I've never had a reason to. I mean, it is not my first thought to go there for my shopping. I just go to the local shop, outta habit I guess.

The direct observational data of the High Street supports this analysis as I was able to capture long-term residents' tacit practices of ignoring Little Poland:

> As I stand along the High Street my attention turns to the local Polish food shop – Little Poland. Despite the hussle and bussle of the High Street, I couldn't help but think why so many member residents were just walking past the store. Perhaps these were long-term residents actively resisting the diversification of the High Street or perhaps they just need not go in. In fact, the only time I saw a residents enter the shop was when I strolling up the High Street and observed a Polish couple enter, after overhearing something that they had said to each other in Polish as I passed by.
>
> (Field note taken from the High Street, 19/9/13)

Under the proposed plans for regeneration, Little Poland was intended to be moved from its current position in the middle of the High Street to an alleyway in between the local jewellers and local estate agents (see Figure 7.1). The reason for the relocation of Little Poland was due to the economic rules of supply and demand: that is, its purpose and function on the High Street were no longer viable. After all, High Streets are sites of public space where the position of shop frontages is contingent upon the sufficient delivery of their particular service to the customer. The relocation was therefore used as Little Poland was not meeting the demand of the wider community of Brickington. Inevitably, this made Kara feel a sense of isolation:

> Now most people that walk past the shop are local people...They'd see my shop, notice its selling ethnic food, and just keep walking. I became really isolated because I wasn't getting any customers.

The relocation of Little Poland, however, became a bit of a double-edged sword in that by relocating Little Poland on the grounds of economics, Kara also felt excluded by, to use the words of Cloke (2004: 33), '*invisibilising the difference*' of Little Poland as it did not represent the cultural traditions and customs of Brickington:

> I had a meeting the other day, with the planning committee. I was shocked with their idea of moving Little Poland to the alley behind (the Jewellers). I almost broke down into tears. I asked

why and all they said was that there's plans for a cake shop. I should have put my foot down but I was too upset. I wonder if I wasn't Polish, would it be the same?

Figure 7.1 – Relocation of Little Poland

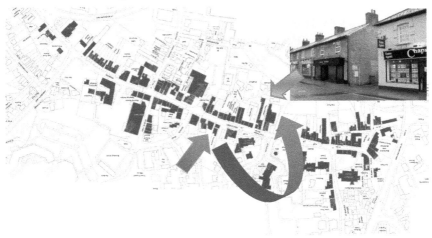

Taken from Brickington Neighbourhood Plan (2012)

These feelings of exclusion, nevertheless, expressed by Kara were largely subjective; that is something that she perceived to be an attack on her Polish identity when in actuality my conversations with other, longer-term residents revealed that this was not the case. For instance, Jane talked about the economic troubles of her business and the town's planning group's proposition of relocation:

> Well, at this very moment we have our own business in the High Street, but I don't know how much longer it is going to last. My husband and I aren't making a profit from it and I know the town team are eying up the shop for relocation. I don't mind relocating as long as the space gets used.

Effectively then, what the data is suggesting is that Kara is linking the coincidence of the relocation of Little Poland with her Polish identity; thus, seeing the relocation as a form of racism. However, Kara's experience of racism was by, and large idiosyncratic as reasons for the relocation of Little Poland were not that much different from that of Jane's shop. Nevertheless, because of the subjectivity of Kara's feelings they did have a very real impact on her sense of belonging to Brickington.

Conclusion

I began this chapter by demonstrating the wider narratives and concerns around the enactment of informal social control in Brickington. The thrust of this discussion was to unpack the exclusionary consequences of informal social control in the way some long-term residents attempted to protect Brickington's rural identity from social change. The data in the first part of this chapter highlighted how the enactment of informal social control reinforced a community that was exclusive and exclusionary, where some of those residents with middle-class status and longer-standing had shared values which allowed them to have the greatest investment into Brickington's specific rural identity.

From here, the chapter sought to explore the experiences of racism faced by some minority ethnic residents, which occurred through actively challenging the legitimacy of different identities, internalised assimilation, or by aversive techniques, such as the relocation of Little Poland and the real and imagined emotional and psychological impact this had on minority ethnic people living in Brickington. In terms of the impact on minority ethnic individuals, I maintained that these feelings of racism resulted from the cumulative effect of active and passive informal social control that sought to regulate the spatial and social boundaries of Brickington in order to protect its specific rural identity (see Chapter 6). In the concluding chapter, I want to discuss the central themes of the book. Further considerations will also be given to the significance of this book in relation to government policy and wider global political events as well as the ways the arguments made throughout this book can be used to inform a forward-looking research agenda and have an impact on 'real world' policy moving forwards into a post-Brexit Britain.

Chapter 8

Conclusion & Implications

Introduction

I began this book with a discussion around Brexit and how the startling result of the EU Referendum on 23 June 2016 needed explaining. How could a relatively wealthy nation with a fairly decent and stable state system act against its political and economic interests as a forward-looking globally connected, and ethnically and culturally diverse country? The answer was a simple one. Globalisation and the almost uncomfortable pace around which change (e.g., uncontrollable migration, supranational governance, the filtering down of power and responsibilities to local communities, greater individualism, cheap air travel, and trade liberalisation) is happening has threatened the power of the nation-state and of nationhood and national identity. The vote for Brexit, therefore, was worked up and constructed as an act of resistance: a push-back against not only continuous migrations which were perceived as diminuting British nationhood but also against cosmopolitanism, elitist politicians and experts – individuals and processes that were perceived as advocating for the expansion of a global, corpocratic multiculture which ignored and flouted the lived realities and experiences of the everyday British public.

What this book has unpacked is that the 'threatened identity from globalisation' narrative which was drawn upon and used to justify Britain's withdrawal from the EU is relational to the concept of rurality and is being played out in the English countryside. The project data that has been discussed and examined throughout this book all reflect this. Such narratives were also there in the anxious, 'age of grief' arguments of the English countryside put forward by Roger Scruton, Paul Kingsnorth, and Roger Askwith (as well as others long before them such as Stanley Baldwin and J.B. Priestley). In some ways what I would suggest is that there is a need to engage with the optics of the global-local relationship of social change within the rural social sciences – to a much greater extent than has (with a few exceptions) been done before (see Woods, 2012, for instance).

In this concluding chapter, my intention is to recursively return and review some of the threads that have run through the previous discussions in other chapters. At its heart, this chapter is concerned with a holistic examination of the impact of social change on the loss of rural identity and increasing ontological insecurity, and the ways in which informal social control is enacted to resist change and protect rural identity to the exclusion of diverse people and processes. The chapter is structured around three broad sections. The first provides a summative reflection of the themes that have arisen through the discussions had in this book. The second explores the significance of this book in terms of debates around the global-local relationship of Brexit and rurality as well as the fallacy of the UK government's rhetoric of 'Shared Society'; and lastly, I will take stock of what the findings and discussions had within this book can do in providing 'real world' policy change and implications for rural areas moving forwards into a post-Brexit Britain. It is to the first section that I now turn to.

Key themes of the book

The conversations had throughout this book have given rise to two distinctive themes: (i) social change, loss of rural identity and ontological insecurity, and (ii) protection of rural identity and the exclusionary outcomes of informal social control. Below I want to offer a final discussion around these two different, but relatable themes to provide a succinct as possible roundup to the book.

Social change, loss of rural identity and ontological insecurity

The first theme drawn out of this book are the worries and anxieties about events, changes, processes, and practices in rural spaces and the English countryside. It was possible to see these anxieties in a number of the interviews – whether it was worries about local social change; about newcomers or about plans to build more homes - that have already been cited in the previous chapters (see Chapters 5, 6 and 7). There is certainly something of this idea of a crisis going on in the current literature around the English countryside also. This is framed as a crisis of loss of identity, and as I have demonstrated this is nothing new. For example, Priestly's (1939) fears about the loss of pastoral England sound very similar to the erosion of the English countryside Kingsnorth (2005) talked about (see Chapter 3 for more details).

These arguments about the insecurities of contemporary rural society were discussed in Chapter 3 in relation to the continuing appeal of the English countryside. When Bauman (2001: 144) argues that 'we miss community because we miss security, a quality crucial to a happy life, but one which the world we inhabit is ever less able to offer and ever more reluctant to promise' it is possible to see the English countryside working as a spatialised expression of the same social needs to which the idea of community appears to be able to provide. There was something of this convergence taking place in the discussions in Chapter 5 where I examined the Brickington carnival as a way of maintaining local identity. This was driven not by a notion of community *per se* but more by the notion of what some residents imagined to be happening – or should be happening – within Brickington. Thus, the anxieties about local change and the erosion of Brickington identity are anxieties not only about what anchors identity in a multi-ethnic, globally located, internationally aligned, nationally devolved social world but perhaps a deeper emotional attachment and sense of loss – what exactly is there left if the imagined landscapes of Brickington and the social relations that go with it disappear altogether from view?

Williams (1979) argues that the English countryside (although he makes the point that urban backstreets also work in this way) is often associated with childhood and of an ideal and 'idea of childhood' and by extension this association of particular geographies with childhoods means that they are inflected by this sense of loss and nostalgia. But there is an association between the English countryside and memory and freedom and safety which both Valentine (2000) and Jones (1997) have examined, and there is something of this captured in Priestley's (1939: xii-xiii) account of what a day out in the English countryside was like when his mother, father or older sister asked.

Similarly then, it is no coincidence that the routine activities of some long-term residents and the implementation of the 'Neighbourhood Plan' was all about a rejection of social change and capturing the traditional look and feel of Brickington, whilst also attempting to preserve the sociality of its residents. For Williams (1979: 358) all this is about structures of feeling in which the experience of change, distance, alienation, are about moving to 'modes of using and consuming rather than accepting and enjoying people and things'.

It is within this context of loss and change that Brickington identity became a potent shorthand for security and timelessness. As chapters 5, 6 and 7 of this book have illustrated this shorthand is able to work effectively and in interconnected ways across both social and spatial levels. Part of this effectiveness is embedded within – and requires – processes in which notions of community and the English countryside are being continually folded. Integral to the arguments as to the uncertainties, fragmentations, and senses of precariousness that constitute the core features of life in Brickington is the suggestion that this produces defensive forms of social retreat and regulation. In a world where, as some commentators (see, for example, Young, 2007; Bauman, 2000; 2001) have argued, western societies have become more entrenched, punitive and exclusive and less public, civic, and tolerant of difference, rule-breaking, transgression and dissent there is an emphasis on the extremes of social organisation – on control, legislation, punishment, imprisonment, cultural recognition, sameness, closed boundaries, and the essentialisation of identities. And if Brickington gets filtered through these arguments, it is possible to see the ways in which the anxieties of the contemporary world can be mapped onto and materially affect what is happening in the place.

Protection of rural identity and exclusionary outcomes of informal social control

As ontological insecurity – and the search for ontological security – intensifies then certain spaces and actions become particularly asserted, valorised and defended as representing the sought-after site of security and reassurance (Neal, 2009). There are two ways in which I would suggest that this ontological insecurity and the search for ways in which to effectively manage it manifest themselves within the English countryside. The first is through worries about social change and the use of action to protect local rural heritage. Chapter 6 examined this when I discussed Brickington's 'Neighbourhood Plan' and how senses of fear and perceptions about a break down in the 'traditional' rural identity of the locality gave rise to local desires of protection to Brickington identity.

For long-term residents, the 'Neighbourhood Plan' was a response to the precarious threats of social change. These 'threats' were conceived as urban dangers coming into the countryside, such as housing expansion, neoliberal businesses and the diversification of the local population. Second, there is a heightened sense that, while being in the countryside does provide some security, this is fragile, uncertain and liable to become less so as threats intrude. Therefore, the local routine activities of residents also get filtered into the maintenance of identity. I offered an account of this in Chapter 5 where the local routines around the carnival provided a sense of a 'traditional' rural identity for long-term residents. Imagery on the floats during the procession as well as how the event was organised and by whom all constituted to Brickington's overall sense of 'rurality'.

From the work cited in this book that has been done within sociology, criminology, human geography as well as rural studies it is clear that the English countryside has been mobilised as a purified space of 'rurality'. There is now also an extensive body of mainly small scale, qualitative oriented research (e.g., Plastow, 2011; Neal, 2009; 2002; Nye, 2006; Hetherington, 2006; Chakraborti and Garland, 2006; 2004; De Lima. 2001; Nizhar, 1995; Derbyshire, 1994; Jay, 1992) which documents and charts the widespread experiences of exclusions within rural areas, specifically exclusionary forms of racism and the various policy and rural agencies' uncertainties as to how to respond to this, and to the notion of multicultural, multi-ethnic populations existing in rural areas. This research has tended to explore hostile and violent forms of hate and discrimination (see Chakraborti and Garland, 2004, specifically); but has also, in recent years examined more insidious and incremental forms of exclusion. For example, in Chapter 7 I highlighted how Tyler's (2006) research in Greenville, a village suburb of Leicester found that the white middle-class village residents tended to speak of how affluent South Asian village residents chose not be part of the community and isolated themselves because they did not join in the activities and neighbourly networks that acted to confirm the idea of Greenville as a caring village continually. The findings of Tyler resonate with the findings made in Chapter 7 about the unattainability of 'fitting in' expressed by some minority ethnic newcomers. This unattainability of 'fitting in' with the wider Brickington community was expressed most clearly by Faseeh and Marie, who indicated how their perceived differences prevented them from joining in with local activities. However, what Chapter 7 also highlighted was that 'fitting in' was achievable for some residents but this was only partial and consisted of suppressing their own identity in order to take on board the wider Brickington identity. Thus, whilst Brickington on the surface appeared to be an inclusive, caring town; below the surface, inclusion into local life for minority ethnic newcomers was more about assimilation than it was integration and cohesion.

Significances of the book

The conversations had throughout this book also have two key significances on current geopolitical events and UK government policy. Firstly, the book has demonstrated that there is a global-local relationship between Brexit and rurality in that the same processes (e.g., globalisation and the resistance to change) which led Britain voting 52-48 percent in favour of leaving the EU are happening within and have an impact on the English countryside. Secondly, this book has highlighted the mythologised nature of Theresa May's 'Shared Society' (and David Cameron's 'Big Society' before that) agenda. Under the 'Shared Society' agenda, the government is giving power to local communities while simultaneously telling them to diversify and embrace difference. But what happens when local communities enact power to protect who they are in a way the government does not want them to do? It is this contradictory fallacy of 'Shared Society' which has been central to the discussions and findings exhibited throughout this book and which I want to come onto and unpack in a little while but before that I would like to begin this section by unpacking and cementing the global-local relationship between Brexit and rurality in a bit more detail.

Brexit and rurality: a global-local relationship

One of the central significances of this book has been the demonstration of how Brexit (the socio-political retreat of the UK from the European Union) as a way to control borders to protect and maintain British identity from immigrants are being played out in a local, rural context. In Chapters 1 and 2 I observed that while globalisation has increased the degrees and types of connectivity in the world as a result of economic restructuring, political reordering, trans and international companies and organisations, multiculture, continuing migrations, technological communications, cheap air travel, it has not subsumed or diminished the idea of nation states or ushered in a monolithic, global culture. In many ways, I argue that it has done the opposite as the British population has increasingly looked to notions of nationhood as a way of creating or maintaining ontological certainties in the face of global crises such as the Syrian refugee crisis and the 'infiltration' of the Islamic State into Europe.

When such perceptions of uncertainty and change are strong, then the process of calling on national identity is acuter. National identity appears to offer a set of shared bonds that precedes the political turbulence that throws up new nations and buries old ones. National identity has pre-modern and almost organic associations; and national identity can offer senses of ontological certainty and reassurance in the face of insecurity and change.

Certainly then, as this book has demonstrated, the discourses around British national identity being in a precarious position in an ever increasing and homogenising globally connected world, do indeed echo the worries of commentators like Kingsnorth (2005; 2011) and Ashwith (2007) discussed in Chapter 3 which testify to the similar senses of the endangerment of rural identity. It is through such discourses in which we can see the iterative and recursive relationship of the global-local. The local – in this context – was the rural nature and character of Brickington which became re-emphasised and valorised due to threats from wider social and spatial pressures such as urbanisation, population diversity, and neoliberalism, while the global can be understood as national threats of migration and the use of Brexit to reclaim British national identity. And for Kingsnorth (2011: 15) the rural local and British global are endlessly folded into the other, and it is a 'commitment to place and to culture [that] can provide a bulwark against the advance of the global consumer machine'.

The 'Shared Society' myth

The second significance of this book is that it has highlighted the contradictory nature of Theresa May's 'Shared Society' agenda. On the one hand, 'Shared Society' is telling rural communities to diversify and build more houses. These *'from above'* policies about diversification and urbanisation are what gets filtered into the turbulences, contentions, and uncertainties of local rural areas and create specific micro-locational anxieties and fear. Such micro-locational fears and anxieties generate a perceived awareness of the loss of local rural identity that enhances greater informal social control. The community dynamics of Brickington meant that informal social control took two forms towards resisting social change. First, the importance of local identity, long-standing and community activities and events were emphasised; and second, community action and the pursuits of 'active citizens'.

This latter point highlights the paradoxical of 'Shared Society'. 'Shared Society' fails to acknowledge that communities are not just people who share a geographic area, but people who have numerous and varied identities. Therefore, and following on from Goffman's (1966) articulation that communities are places where identities are learned, constructed, practiced and maintained and acted out, this book has highlighted the fallacy of Theresa May's 'Shared Society' rhetoric. That is, on the one hand, it is advocating increased localism to promote stronger, cohesive communities; whilst, on the other hand, such policies create community spaces where rural identities are acted out and produce exclusive and exclusionary rural communities of vested interest, common identity and shared values.

This was evidenced in Brickington by the 'Neighbourhood Plan': a community-led response to a local social change in the area that was seen as threatening to its rural identity and character. The 'Neighbourhood Plan' demonstrates that why it was logical of the government to believe that the more involved communities are in the organisation, running and maintenance of their local area, the stronger and more integrated those places will become. What the government did not perceive – and this is where the primary failing of the 'Shared Society' agenda is – is that when given increased power communities will not use it to protect assets of community value (e.g., community centres, pubs, local swimming pools), which is what the government had hoped, but rather local communities will use their devolved power to protect and maintain the vested interest of those with the greatest sense of community, consequentially excluding all those newcomers from belonging, and where minority ethnic newcomers are doubly at risk of experiencing feelings of exclusion and racism.

'Real world' policy implications

The findings from this book demonstrate that more needs to be done to develop a policy that addresses the real-life issues facing rural areas, and the UK more generally heading into a post-Brexit Britain, to address the underlying theme of communities in change. Government policy appears to be blind to the apprehension of globalisation amongst the public. People are threatened by change as there is a perception that continuous migrations, the growth of online connectivity and the expansion of neoliberalism may lead to the death of community. The current rhetoric and discourse within the rural studies literature (e.g., Woods, 2012; Shucksmith, in press) is that communities feel *left behind* by globalisation, as though they want to wholeheartedly embrace change and be reconnected with the rest of the world. However, this is not the case. What the findings from this study have shown is that local people do not feel *left behind* by globalisation, but rather feel *let down* by government policy which they perceive to be advocating the expansion of a global, corporate, multiculture while ignoring the local and regional identities of 'settled' rural communities.

The 'Shared Society' agenda attempted to address this issue by creating greater cohesive rural communities through increased civic engagement by devolving power to local areas. This, however, has only helped mitigate the impact of change on rural communities so far. Ultimately, the 'Shared Society' agenda has encouraged rural communities where those longer-term residents with the greatest attachment to their area will actively look for ways to maintain and protect their identity at the risk of creating exclusive and exclusionary communities of vested interests, rather than finding local solutions to strengthening rural identity while also recognising the value of social change.

The recommendations for future policy, therefore, of which this book throws up is that governmental debates around the social change in the English countryside need to include more explicit discussions about better ways to balance the protection of local rural identity with the promotion of change. At the moment, increased localism under the 'Shared Society' agenda is not working as well as it should be in creating this balance. There needs to be a renewing of the centre to help facilitate the balance between top-down government policy and local/regional power. More research needs to be done to explore the possible ways in which to achieve a) a better policy agenda that encourages the integration of national and local and regional governance and b) central compatibility between endorsing the benefits of change to rural areas and alleviating local fears about loss of rural identity by strengthening rural identity.

This centrist approach to policy is more pertinent than ever given the current socio-political climate. The result of the 2016 EU referendum has become a sure sign that we are now living in an age of ontological uncertainty. Emotion and insecurities around particularly threatened identities seem to run the roost above the plight of policy-making. In fact, rural Britain was home to one of the biggest proportion of individuals who decided to leave the European Union on 23 June 2016, and it is within these rural communities where social divisions derived from fear are most acute as many rural areas latch onto tradition and the protection of their way of life. On the face of it, this romanticism of the English countryside may appear tame, but below the surface, as this book has highlighted, it has potential to create exclusive and exclusionary boundaries (Sibley, 1997). Such exclusionary consequences can only breed further division and atomisation. It is important, therefore, to begin engaging in an open dialogue and debate about the possible ways to better integrate the protection of rural identities with the promotion of social change before further divisions manifest with the rise of the Populist Right across the English countryside and elsewhere.

Final thoughts

The purpose of this book was to explore long-term residents' perceptions of globalisation as a threat to the specific identity of an English rural town, and how the community dynamics and socio-spatial organisation of daily life reinforced the notion of a rural idyll to the exclusion of processes and people seen as representing different and diverse identities, values and ideals. I have highlighted the impact globalisation had on Brickington identity as well as the relationship between people's actions to maintain and protect the specific rural identity of the place with the similar processes that led to the British public voting to leave the EU. While this book is relatively small-scale I hope it has raised some pertinent points and questions about the context specific dynamics of identity, particularly the local-contextual nature of feelings of ontological insecurity, informal social control and their implications on racism in a rural context and how these are influenced by and give rise to bigger, global tensions and concerns about nationhood and the turbulent nature of British national identity and how people are seeking ways in which to secure and anchor their identities from the problems and issues globalisation has thrown up for individuals, communities, and nations within the 21st Century.

References

Abrams, S. A. (2003) 'Gazing on Rurality'. in *Country Visions*. ed. by Cloke, P. Harlow: Pearson, 32-48.

Allan, G. and Crow, G. (1989). 'Introduction'. In *Home and Family: Creating the Domestic Sphere*. Ed by. Allan, G. and Crow, G. Basingstoke: Macmillan, 1-13.

Adler, P. A., and Adler, P. (2000). 'Observational techniques'. In. *Handbook of Qualitative Research*. Ed by. Denzin, N.K.; & Lincoln, Y.S. Thousand Oaks: Sage, 377-392.

Adler, P. and Adler, P. (1987) *Membership Roles in Field Research*. Newbury Park: Sage.

Alleyne, B. (2002) 'An Idea of Community and its Discontents: Towards a More Reflexive Sense of Belonging in Multicultural Britain.' *Ethnic and Racial Studies* 25 (4), 607-627.

Allport, G. (1979) *The Nature of Prejudice*. New York: Basic Books.

Altheide, D. L. and Johnson, J. M. (1998). 'Criteria for assessing interpretive validity in Qualitative Research''. In *Collecting and Interpreting Qualitative Materials*. Ed. by Denzin, N. K. and Lincoln, Y. S. Thousand Oaks: Sage, 283-313.

Amit, V. and Rapport, N. (2002) *The Trouble with Community: Anthropological Reflections on Movement, Identity and Collectivity*. London: Pluto Press.

Anderson, B. (2006) *Imagined Communities: Reflections on the Origin and Spread of Nationalism*. London: Verso.

Arber, S. (1993) 'The Research Process'. In *Researching Social Life*. Ed. by Gilbert, N. London: Sage, 32-50.

Arensberg, C. and Kimball, S. (1940) *Family and Community in Ireland*. County Clare: Clasp Press.

Arksey, H. and Knight, P. (1999) *Interviewing for Social Scientists*. London: Sage.

Ary, D., Jacobs, L., Sorenson, C., and Walker, D. (2013) *Observational Research in the Social Sciences*. London: Wadsworth.

Askwith, K. (2007) *The Lost Village: In Search of a Forgotten Rural England*. London: Ebury Press.

Asselin, M. E. (2003) 'Insider Research: Issues to Consider when Conducting Research in Your Own Setting'. Journal of Nurses in Staff Development 19 (2), 99-103.

Atkinson, R. and Flint, J. (2003). 'Order Born of Chaos? The Capacity for Informal Social Control in Disempowered and 'Disorganised' Neighbourhoods'. In *Policy & Press*, 32 (3), 333-335

Banton, M. (1983). *Racial and Ethnic Competition*. Cambridge: Cambridge University Press.

Barth, F. (1969) *Ethnic Groups and Boundaries*. Boston: Little Brown.

Bauman, Z. (2001) *Community: Seeking Safety in an Insecure World*. Cambridge: Polity.

Bauman, Z. (2000) *Liquid Modernity*. Cambridge: Polity.

Beck, U. (1992) *Risk Society: Towards a New Modernity*. London: Sage.

Becker, H. (1963) *Outsiders: Studies in the Sociology of Deviance*. New York: Free Press.

Bell, M. (1994) *Childerley: Nature, and Morality in an English Village*. London: University of Chicago Press.

Bell, C. and Newby, H. (1979) 'The Fruit of Difference: The Rural Divide in Postmodern Britain'. *Journal of Sociology* 17 (2), 16-25

Bell, C., and Newby, H. (1971) *Community Studies: An Introduction to the Sociology of the Local Community*. *London*: Allen and Unwin.

Benedict, R. (2006). *The Chrysanthemum and the Sword*. First published in 1949. New York: Mariner Books.

Benson, R. (2005). *The Farm*. London: Hamish Hamilton.

Bhattacharyya, G. (1999). 'Teaching race in cultural studies: a ten-step programme of personal development'. In *Ethnic and Racial Studies Today*. Ed by Bulmer, M. and Solomos, J. London: Routledge.

Billig, M. (2002). *Banal Nationalism*. London: Sage.

Black, D. (1976). T*he Behaviour of Law*. New York: Academic Press.

Blunden, J. and Curry, N. (1988) *A Future for our Countryside*. London: Routledge.

Bocock, R. (1974) *Ritual in Rural Society*. London: Allen & Unwin.

Bondi, L., Davidson, J. and Smith, M. (2005). 'Geography's 'Emotional Turn''. In *Emotional Geographies*. Ed by Davidson, J., Bondi, L. and Smith, M.. Aldershot: Ashgate.

Bottoms, A.; Baldwin, J and Walker, M. (1976). *Urban Criminal: A Study in Sheffield*. London: Tavistock.

Bourdieu, P. (1986) 'The Forms of Capital'. in *Handbook of Theory and Research for the Sociology of Education*. ed. by Richardson, J. New York: Greenwood.

Bowling, B. (1998) *Violent Racism: Victimisation, Policing and Social Context*. Oxford: Oxford University Press.

Braithwaite, J. (1989) *Crime, Shame and Reintegration*. Cambridge: Cambridge University Press.

Brannick, T. and Coghlan, D. (2007). 'In the Defence of being 'Native''. *Organisational Research Methods* 10 (1), 59-74.

Braun, V., and Clare, V. (2013). *Successful Qualitative Research: a practical guide for beginners*. Sage: London

Braun, V., and Clarke, V. (2006) 'Using Thematic Analysis in Psychology'. *Qualitative Research in Psychology* 3(2), 77-101.

Bressey, C. (2009). 'Cultural archaeology and historical geographies of the black presence in rural England'. In *Journal of Rural Studies* 25(4), 386-395.

Breuer, F. and Roth, M. W. (2003) 'Subjectivity and Reflexivity in the Social Sciences: epistemic windows and methodical consequences'. *Qualitative Social* Research 4(3), 335-359.

Brickington Neighbourhood Planning Group (2012). *Brickington Neighbourhood Plan.* [online] available from https://www.dorsetforyou.gov.uk/405456.

British National Party (2002). *Britain's Destiny: The New Atlantis?* [online] available from //www. landand-people. oriz/at] antis extinction.htm

Browning, C.R.; Feinberg, S.L. and Dietz, R.D. (2004). 'The Paradox of Social Organization: Networks, Collective Efficacy, and Violent Crime in Urban Neighbourhoods.' in *Social Forces.* 83 (2), 503-534.

Bryman, A. (1988) Quantity and Quality in Social Research. London: Routledge.

Bulmer, M. (1982). 'The merits and demerits of covert participant observation'. In *Social research ethics.* Ed by. Bulmer, M. London: Macmillan, 217-251.

Bunce, M. (1994) *The Countryside Ideal: Anglo-American Images of Landscape.* London: Routledge.

Burchfield, K. (2009) 'Attachment as a Source of Informal Social Control in an Urban Neighbourhood'. *Journal of Criminal Justice* 37 (1), 45-54.

Burgess, R. G. (1982) 'Approaches to Field Research'. In *Field Research: a sourcebook and field manual.* Ed. by Burgess, R. G. London: Unwin Hyman, 1-11.

Calhoun, C. (2016). 'Brexit Is a Mutiny Against the Cosmopolitan Elite'. In *New Perspectives Quarterly* 33, 50–58

Campbell, D. (2006). 'Geopolitics and visuality: Sighting the Darfur conflict'. Available at http://doi:10.1016/j.polgeo [accessed 15 January 2017].

Cante, T. (2005) *Community Cohesion: A New Framework for Race and Diversity.* Basingstoke: Palgrave Macmillan.

Chakraborti, N.; and Garland, J. (2007) 'Protean Times: exploring the relationship between policing, community and 'race' in rural England'. *Criminology & Social Justice* 7 (4), 347-365

Chakraborti, N. (2007) *Warm Beer and Invincible Green Suburbs'? Examining the Realities of Rurality for Minority Ethnic Households.* Unpublished PhD thesis or dissertation. Leicester: University of Leicester.

Chakraborti, N. and Garland, J. (2006) 'Race, Space and Place: Examining Cultures of Exclusion in Rural England'. *Journal of Ethnic and Racial Studies* 86 (1), 931-957.

Chakraborti, N. and Garland, J. (2004) *Rural Racism.* London: Willan.

Chavez, S. (2005) 'Community and Ethnicity in a Changing Rural English Town'. *Journal of Rural Sociology* 70 (3), 314-335.

Chriss, J. (2007). *Social Control: An Introduction.* London: Polity Press

Christians, C. (2000) 'Ethics and Politics in Qualitative Research'. In Handbook of Qualitative Research. Ed. by Denzin, N. K. and Lincoln, Y. S. Thousand Oaks: Sage, 133-155.

Clarke, J. (2009) *ERSC Policing in an Age of Diversity.* 'Fantasies of Community and Community as Governance' at University of Leicester: Leicester.

Cloke, P. (2004) 'Rurality and Racialised Others: Out of Place in the Countryside'. In *Rural Racism.* Ed. by Chakraborti, N. and Garland, J. London: Willian, 17-35.

Cloke, P. (1997) 'Country Blackwater to Virtual Village? Rural Studies and the 'Cultural Turn'. *Journal of Rural Studies* 13 (4), 367-375.

Cloke, P. and Little, J. (1997) *Contested Countryside Cultures: Otherness, Marginalisation and Rurality.* London: Routledge.

Cloke, P. (1992) 'The Countryside Development: Conservation and an Increasingly Marketedable Commodity'. In *Policy and Change in Thatcher's Britain.* Ed. by Cloke, P. Oxford: Pergamon, 269-295

Cloke, P. and Milbourne, P. (1992) ''Deprivation and Lifestyles in Rural Wales'. *Journal of Rural Studies,* 8 (4), 359-371.

Cloke, P. (1977) 'An Index of Rurality for England and Wales'. *Journal of Regional Studies* 20, 31-46.

Cochrane, A. and Talbot, D. (2008) *Security: Welfare, Crime and Society.* Maidenhead: Open University Press.

Cohen, A. (1985a) *Symbolising Boundaries: Identity and Diversity in British Cultures.* Manchester: Manchester University Press.

Cohen, A. (1985b) *The Symbolic Construction of Community.* London: Routledge.

Cohen, A. (1982). *Belonging, Identity and Social Organisation in British Rural Cultures.* Manchester: Manchester University Press.

Commission of Rural Communities (2012). *Commission for Rural Communities annual report.* London: Commission for Rural Communities.

Connerton, P. (1989) *How Society Remembers.* Cambridge: Cambridge University Press.

Connolly, P. (2006) 'It Goes without Saying (Well Sometimes): Racism, Whiteness and Identity'. *International Journal of Rural Studies* 20 (3), 21-47.

County Council. (2011). *Brickington demography.* [online] available from https://apps.geowessex.com/stats/AreaProfiles/Town/gillingham.

Cumming, D. and Johan, S. (2010). 'The differential impact of the internet on spurring on regional entrepreneurship'. *Entrepreneurship Theory & Practice* 34 (5), 857-883.

Crawford, A. (2003). "Contractual Governance' of Deviant Behaviour'. *Journal of Law & Criminal Justice,* 30 (4), 479-505.

Creswell, J. W. (2003) Research Design. London: Sage

Creswell, J. W. (1998). *Qualitative Inquiry and Research Design: choosing among five traditions.* Thousand Oaks: Sage.

Crotty, M. (1998) *The Foundations of Social Research: meaning and perspective in the research process.* London: Sage.

Crowley, C., Harre, R., and Tagg, C. (2002). 'Qualitative Research and Computing: Methodological Issues in using ORS NVivo'. *International Journal of Social Research Methodology* 5(3), 193-197.

Daniels, S. and Cosgrove, D. (1993) 'Spectacle and Text: Landscape Metaphors in Cultural Geography.' In *Place, Culture and Representations*. Ed. by Duncan, S. and Ley, D. London: Routledge, 57-77.

Dargan, L. and Shucksmith, M. (2008). 'LEADER and innovation'. *Sociologia Ruralis*, 48 (3), 274-291.

Davis, M. (2005) *Planet of Slums*. London: Verso.

Davis, S. G. (1986) *Parades and Power: street theatre in the Nineteenth Century*. Philadelphia: Temple University Press.

Day, G. (2006) *Community in Everyday Life*. London: Routledge.

Debord, G. (1973). *The Society of the Spectacle*. Detroit: Black and Red.

DEFRA. (2011). *Rural-Urban Classification*. London: DEFRA.

De Lima, P. (2008) *Ethnicity, 'Race' and Place: Experiences and Issues of Identity and Belonging in Rural Minority Ethnic Households*. Unpublished PhD thesis or dissertation: University of Stirling: Stirling.

De Lima, P. (2001) *Needs Not Numbers: An Exploration of Ethnic Minorities Communities in Scotland*. London: Commission for Racial Equality and Community Development Foundation.

DeMunck, V. C. and Sobo, E. J. (1998). *Using Methods in the Field*. California: AltaMira Press.

Denzin, N. K. and Lincoln, Y. S. (2000). 'Methods of Collecting and Analysing Empirical Materials'. In *Handbook of Qualitative Research*. Ed. by Denzin, N. K. and Lincoln, Y. S. Thousand Oaks: Sage, 633-643.

Derbyshire, H. (1994) *Not in Norfolk: Tackling the Invisibility of Racism*. Norfolk: Norwich and Norfolk Racial Equality Council.

Derounian, J. G. (1993) *Another Country: Real Life Beyond Rose Cottage*. London: NCVO.

Dewalt, K. M., and Dewalt, B. R. (2002). *Participant observation: A guide for fieldworkers*. New York: AltaMira.

DeWalt, K. M. and Dewalt, B. R. (1998). 'Direct Observation'. In *Handbook of Methods in Cultural Anthropology*. Ed. by Bernard, R. Walnut Creek: AltaMira, 259-300.

Dingwall, R. (1980). 'Ethics and ethnography.' *The Sociological Review*, 28, 871-891.

Donnermeyer, J. (2015) 'The Social Disorganisation of the Rural and Identity in the UK; Conceptual Considerations'. *Journal of Rural Studies* 84 (2), 26-41.

Dozier, R. W. (2002) *Why we Hate*. New York: Contemporary Books.

Duneier, M. (2005) *Slim's Table: Race, Respectability and Masculinity*. Chicago & London: University of Chicago Press.

Dupuis, A. and Thorns, D.C. (1998). 'Home, home ownership and the search for ontological security'. In *Sociological Review*, 46 (1), 24-47.

Durkheim, E. (2014) *The Division of Labour in Society*. First published in 1893. New York: Free Press.

Edwards, A. and Hughes, G. (2005). 'Comparing the Governance of Safety in Europe: A Geo-Historical Approach.' *Theoretical Criminology* 9 (3), 345–363.

Edwards, S.I. and Bruce, C. (2002). 'Reflective internet searching: an action research model.' *The Learning Organisation*, 9(4), 180-188.

Elson, M. (1986) *Green Belts: Conflict Mediation in the Urban Fringe*. London: Heinesman.

Esuantsiwa Goldsmith, J. and Makris, M. (1994) *Staring at Invisible Women: Black and Minority Ethnic Women in Rural Areas*. London: National Alliance of Women's Organisation.

Featherstone, M. (1992). *Consumer Culture and Postmodernism*. Sage: London.

Fenton, S. (1999). *Ethnicity, Racism, Class and Culture*. London: Macmillan.

Fielding, N. (1993) 'Ethnography'. In *Researching Social Life*. Ed. by Gilbert, N. London: Sage, 154-171.

Fish, R. (2000) *Putting Together Rurality: Media Producers and the Social Construction of the Countryside*. Unpublished PhD thesis or dissertation: University of Leicester: Leicester.

Foster, J. (1995) 'Informal Social Control and Community Crime Prevention'. *British Journal of Criminology* 35 (4), 563-583.

Foucault, M. (1986) 'Of Other Spaces'. *Diacritics* 16 (1), 22-27.

Foucault, M. (1980) *Knowledge/power*. London: Pantheon Books.

Foucault, M. (1977). *Discipline and Punish: The Birth of the Prison*. London: Allen Lane.

Francis, D. and Henderson, P. (1992) *Working with Rural Communities*. Basingstoke: Macmillan.

Frankenberg, R. (1993). *The Social Construction of Whiteness*. London: Routledge.

Gallent, N. and Robinson, S. (2011) 'Local Perspectives on Rural Housing and its Implications on Localism in Rural England'. *Journal of Rural Studies* 27 (3), 297-307.

Gans, H. J. (1999). 'Participant observation in the era of "ethnography"'. *Journal of Contemporary Ethnography*, 28, 540-548.

Garland, D. (2001). *The Culture of Control: Crime and Social Order in Contemporary Society*. Oxford: Oxford University Press.

Garland, J. and Rowe, M. (2001) *Racism and Anti-racism in Football*. Basingstoke: Palgrave Macmillan

Geertz, C. (1973) *The Interpretation of Cultures*. New York: Basic Books.

Gergen, K. J. (1994) 'The Communal Creation of Meaning'. In *The Nature and Ontogenesis of Meaning*. Ed. by Overton, W. F. New Jersey: Lawrence Erlbaum Associates, 19-40.

Gibson, C. and Connell, J. (2011) *Carnival Spaces*. Bristol: Channel View.

Giddens, A. (2014). *Off the edge of history*. Lecture Series. Held at Canterbury Christ Church University on 18th March

Giddens, A. (2013). *Turbulent and Mighty Continent: what future for Europe?* London: Wiley.

Giddens, A. (2002) *Runaway World*. Cambridge: Cambridge University Press.

Giddens, A. (1991) *Modernity and Self-Identity: Self and Society in the Late Modern Age.* Cambridge: Polity.

Giddens, A. (1984) *The Constitution of Society: Towards a Theory of Structuration.* Cambridge: Polity.

Gilroy, P. (2005) *Postcolonial Melancholia.* London: Columbia University Press.

Gkartzios, M. and Scott, M. (2013) 'Attitudes to Housing, Planning Policy and Population Growth in Rural Localities: Disparities between Long-Term and Mobile Rural Populations in Ireland'. *Land use Policy* 31 (1), 347-357.

Goodwin, M. and Heath, O. (2016). 'The 2016 Referendum, Brexit and the Left Behind: An Aggregate-level Analysis of the Result.' In *The Political Quarterly* 87 (3), 323–332.

Goffman, E. (1999) *The Presentation of Self in Everyday Life.* First published in 1959. London: Peter Smith Publishing.

Goffman, E. (1963) *Stigma: notes on the management of spoiled identity.* London: Penguin.

Goffman, E. (1966) *Behaviour in Public Places: Notes on the Social Organisation of Gatherings.* New York: Free Press.

Gottfredson, M. and Hirschi, T. (1990) *A General Theory of Crime.* Stanford: Stanford University Press.

Gupta, A. and Ferguson, J. (1997) *Culture, Power, Place: Ethnographies at the End of an Era.* North Carolina: Duke University Press.

Habermas, J. (2016). 'Core Europe to the Rescue: A Conversation with Jürgen Habermas about Brexit and the EU Crisis.' [online] available at: https://www.socialeurope.eu/2016/07/core-europe-to-the-rescue/.

Hall, S. (2012). *City, Street, and Citizen: the measure of the ordinary.* Abingdon: Routledge.

Hall, S. (1992). 'The New Ethnicities'. In *Race, Culture and Difference.* Ed by Donald, J. and Rattansi, A. London: Sage.

Halpern, D. (2009) *Social Capital.* Cambridge: Polity.

Halsey, A. H. (1995) *The Decline of Donnish Dominance.* Oxford: Clarendon.

Hammersley, M. and Atkinson, P. (1995) *Ethnography: Principles in Practice.* London: Routledge.

Harvey, D. (1996) *Nature, Justice and the Geographies of Difference.* Massachusetts: Blackwell Press.

Hasenfeld, Y. and Garrows, E. (2012) 'Non-profit Human Service Organisations, Social Rights, and Advocacy in a Neoliberal Welfare State'. *Social Service Review* 86 (2), 295-322.

Heley, J. (2008). 'Rurality, Class, Aspirations and the Emergence of the 'New Squierarchy'. Unpublished PhD. Wales: University of Aberystwyth.

Her Majesty's Government (2010). *The Localism Act (2010).* London: Her Majesty's Government

Hetherington, K. (2006) 'Visions of England: New Age Travellers and the Concept of Ethnicity'. In *The New Countryside? Ethnicity and Exclusion in Contemporary Rural Britain.* Ed. by Neal, S. and Agyeman, J. Milton Keynes: Open University Press, 173-193.

Hetherington, K. (1997) *The Badlands of Modernity.* London: Routledge.

Hirsch, F. (1977) 'Social Limits to Growth'. *The Economic Journal* 87 (347), 574-578.

Hobbs, D. (2002). 'Ethnography and the study of deviance.' In. *Handbook of ethnography.* Ed by Atkinson, P.; Coffey, S.; Delamont, J. & Lofland, L. London: Sage, 204-219.

Holloway, S. L. (2004) 'Rural Roots, Rural Routes: Discourses on Rural Self and the Travelling Other in Debates about the Future of New Appleby Fair'. *Journal of Rural Studies* 20 (2), 143-156.

Homan, R. (1980). 'The ethics of covert methods.' British Journal of Sociology, 31, 46-59

Home Office (2005) *Community Cohesion Agenda.* London: Home Office.

Hope, T. and Foster, J. (1992). 'Conflicting Forces: Changing the Dynamics of Crime and Community on a 'Problem' Estate.' *British Journal of Criminology*, 32 (4), 488-504.

Howkins, A. (1986). 'The discovery of rural England in Englishness'. In *Politics and Culture 1880–1920.* Ed by Colls, R. and Dodd, P. London: Croom Helm.

Hubbard, P. (2006) 'Inappropriate and Incongruous: Opposition to Asylum Seekers in the English Countryside'. *Journal of Rural Studies* 21 (1), 3-17.

Hughes, G. (2007). *The Politics of Crime and Community.* Basingstoke: Palgrave

Hughes, A. and Morris, C. S., S. (2000). 'Introduction'. In *Ethnography and Rural Research.* Ed. by Hughes, A. and Morris, C. S., S. Cheltenham: The Countryside and Community Press, 1-28.

Humphreys, L. (1970). *Tearoom trade.* Chicago: Aldine.

Hutchinson, J. and Smith, A. D. (1996) *Ethnicity.* Oxford University Press: Oxford.

Innes, M. (2003). *Understanding Social Control: Deviance, Crime and Social Order.* Maidenhead: Open University Press.

Jackson, P. (1994). 'Ethnography'. In *The Dictionary of Human Geography.* Ed. by Johnson, R., Gregory, D., and Smith, D. Oxford: Blackwell, 238.

Jackson, A. (1991). *The Middle Classes 1900-1950.* Nairn: David St. John Thomas.

Jackson, A. (ed.) (1987) *Anthropology at Home.* London: Travistock.

James, J. (2014) *The Internet and the Google Age.* Dublin: Research Publishing.

Jay, E. (2000) *Keep them in Birmingham.* London: Commission for Racial Equality.

Jenkins, R. (1997). *Rethinking Nationhood: Arguments and Explorations.* London: Sage.

Jones, O. and Cloke, P. (2001) *Tree Cultures: The Place of Trees and Trees in their Place.* London: Berg.

Jones, O. (1997) 'Little Figures, Big Shadows: Country Childhood Stories'. In *Contested Countryside Cultures.* Ed. by Cloke, P. and Little, J. London: Routledge, 172-195.

Kanuha, V. K. (2000) ''being' Native Versus 'Going Native': Conducting Social Work Research as an Insider'. *Social Work* 45 (5), 439-447.

Kearns, G. (1993) 'The City as Spectacle: Paris and the Hicentenary of the French Revolution.' In *Selling Places: The City as Cultural Capital, Past and Present.* Ed. by Kearns, G. and Philo, C. London: Pergamon, 49-102.

Kendall, S. (2014). *Britain's Lost High Streets: a history of everyday life in our villages, towns and cities.* Amberley: Stroud.

Kenny, M. (2014). *The politics of English nationhood.* Oxford: Oxford University Press.

Kidd, L. and Judd, M. (1986). *Research Methods in Social Relations.* New York: CBS College Publishing.

King, M. and May, C. (1985) *Black Magistrates: A Study of Selection and Appointments.* London: Cobden Trust.

Kingdom, J. (1993) *No such Thing as a Society: Individualism and Community.* Buckingham: Open University Press

Kingsnorth, P. (2011) *Real England: Battle Against the Bland.* London: Wadsworth.

Kingsnorth, P. (2005) *Your Countryside, Your Choice.* Hertfordshire: Campaign to Protect Rural England.

Kinnvall, C. (2004). 'Globalisation and Religious Nationalism: self-identity and the search for ontological security.' In *Political Psychology*, 25 (5), 741-767.

Klein, M. (1986) *Our Adult World and its Roots in Infancy.* London: Heinemann.

Klinger, D. A. (1997) 'Negotiating Order in Patrol Work: an Ecological Theory of Police Response to Deviance'. *Criminology* 35 (2), 277-307.

Kundnami, A. (2007) *The End of Intolerance: Racism in 21st Century Britain.* London: Pluto.

Laurier, E. and Philo, C. (2006). 'Cold shoulders and napkins handed: gestures of responsibility'. *Transactions of the Institute of British Geographers*, 31 (2), 193-208.

Lash, S. and Urry, J. (1994) *Economies of Signs and Space.* London: Sage.

Lea J. and Stenson, K. (2007). 'Security, Sovereignty, and Non-State Governance 'From Below'. In *Canadian Journal of Law and Society*, 22 (2), 9-28.

Lee, R. M. (1993). *Doing research on sensitive topics.* London: Sage

Lefebvre, D. (1991) *The Production of Space.* London: Blackwell.

Lewis, G. and Neal, S. (2005). 'Introduction: Contemporary political contexts, changing terrains and revisited discourses.'. In *Ethnic and Racial Studies* 28(3), 423-444.

Ley, D. and Olds, K. (1988) 'Landscape as Spectacle: World's Fairs and the Culture of Heroic Consumption'. *Society & Space* 6, 191-212.

Little, J. and Austin, P. (1996) 'Rural Geography: Rural Gender Identity and the Performance of Masculinity and Femininity in the Countryside'. *Progress in Human Geography* 26, 665-670.

Locke, L. F., Silverman, S. J., and Spirduso, W. W. (2004). *Reading and Understanding Research.* London: Sage.

Lowe, P., Murdoch, J., Marsden, T., Munton, R., and Flynn, A. (1993) 'Regulating the New Rural Spaces: Uneven Development of Land'. *Journal of Rural Studies* 9 (3), 205-222.

Lowles, N. (2001) *White Riot: The Violent Story of Combat*. Bury: Milo Books.

Lugosi, P. (2006). 'Between Overt and Covert Research: Concealment and Disclosure in an Ethnographic Study of Commercial Hospitality'. *Qualitative Inquiry* 12(3), 531-541.

Mabey, R. (2007) *Nature Cure*. London: Pimlico.

Mac an Ghaill, M. (1999). *Contemporary Racism and Ethnicities: Social and Cultural Transformations. Buckingham*. Open University Press.

Magne, S. (2003) *Multi-Ethnic Devon: A Rural Handbook–The Report of the Devon and Exeter Racial Equality Council's Rural Outreach Project*. Devon: Devon and Exeter Racial Equality Council.

Malcolm, D. (2004) 'Outsiders Within: The Reality of Rural Racism'. In *Rural Racism*. ed. by Chakraborti, N. and Garland, J. London: Wilian, 63-85

Malinowski, B. (2014). *Argonauts of the Western Pacific*. First published in 1922. London: Routledge.

Marston, S. (1989) 'Public Rituals and Community Power: St Patrick's Day Parades in Lowell, Massachusetts'. *Political Geography Quarterly* 8, 232-240.

Massey, D. (1994) *Space, Place and Gender*. Cambridge: Polity Press.

Matless, D. (1994) 'Doing the English Village: An Essay in Imagative Geography'. In *Writing the Rural: Five Cultural Geographies*. Ed. by Cloke, P., Doel. D., Matless, D., Philips, M., and Thrift, N. London: Paul Chapman, 7-88.

McCormick, J. and Jones, C. (1993). 'The Conceptualisation of Deracialisation.' In *Dilemmas of Black Politics*. Ed by Persons, G. New York: Harper Collins, 66-84

McLaughlin, E. and Neal, S. (2007). 'Who can speak to race and nation? Intellectuals, public policy formation and the future of multi-ethnic Britain commission'. In *Cultural Studies* 21(6), 910-930.

MacPherson, W. (1999) *The Stephen Lawrence Inquiry*. London: HMSO.

Midgley, J. (2001) 'The United States: Welfare, Work and Development'. *International Journal of Social Welfare* 10 (4), 284-293.

Milbourne, P. (1997) 'Hidden from View: Poverty and Marginalisation in Rural Britain'. In *Revealing Rural Others: Marginalisation, Otherness and Exclusion*. Ed. by Milbourne, P. London: Routledge, 89-116.

Mooney, G. and Neal, S. (eds.) (2009) *Community, Welfare, Crime and Society*. Milton Keynes: Open University Press.

Mort, F. (1996). Cultures of consumption. Routledge: London.

Moseley, M. and Pahl, R. (2007) *Social Capital in Rural Places*. London: DEFRA.

Mullaly, B. (2007) 'The Social Work Vision: A Progressive View'. In *The New Structural Social Work*. Ed. by Mullaly, B. Canada: Oxford Press, 44-69.

Murdoch, J. and Pratt, A. C. (1997) 'From Topography of Power to Power of Topography'. In *Contested Countryside Cultures: Otherness, Marginalisation and Rurality*. Ed. by Cloke, P. and Little, J. London: Routledge, 51-69.

Murdoch, J. and Pratt, A. (1994). 'Rural Studies of power and the power of rural studies: a reply to Philo'. In *Journal of Rural Studies* 10, 83–87.

Murdoch, J. (2003) 'Co-Constructing the Countryside: Hybrid and the Extensive Self'. In *Country Visions*. Ed. by Cloak, P. Harlow: Pearson, 45-61.

Murdoch, J. and Day, G. (1998) 'Middle Class Mobility, Rural Communities and the Politics of Exclusion. In *Migration into Rural Areas: Theories and Issues*. Ed. by Halfacree, K. H. and Boyle, P. Chichester: Wiley, 186-199.

Murdoch, J. and Marsden, T. (1994) *Reconstituting Rurality: A Changing Countryside in an Urban Context*. London: UCL Press.

Neal, S. (2009) *Rural Identities: Ethnicity and Community in the Contemporary English Countryside*. Surrey: Ashgate.

Neal, S. and Walters, S. (2008) 'Rural be/longing and rural social organisations: conviviality and community-making in the English countryside' *Sociology* 42 (4), 279-293.

Neal, S. and Walters, S. (2006) 'Strangers Asking Strange Questions? A Methodological Narrative on Researching Belonging and Identity in the English Countryside'. *Journal of Rural Studies* 22 (2), 170-188.

Neal, S. and Agyeman, J. (eds) (2006a). *The New Countryside? Ethnicity, Nation and Exclusion in Contemporary Rural Britain*. Bristol: The Policy Press.

Neal, S. and Agyeman, J. (2006b) 'Remaking English Ruralities: Processes of Belonging and Becoming, Continuity and Change in Racialised Spaces'. in *The New Countryside?*. Ed. by Agyeman, J. and Neal, S. Bristol: Polity Press, 99-125.

Newby, H. (1979) *Green and Pleasant Lands: Belonging in the English Countryside*. London: Penguin.

Nizhar, P. (1995) *No Problem? Race Issues in Shropshire*. Telford: Race Equality Forum for Telford and Shropshire.

Nye, M. (2006) *Multiculturalism and Minority Religions in Britain: Krishna Consciousness, Religious Freedom and the Politics of Location'*. Surrey: Curzon Press.

O'Leary, P. (2012) *Claiming the Streets: Procession and Culture in Urban Wales*. Cardiff: University of Wales Press.

Oliver, P., and Jupp, V. (2006) 'Purposive Sampling'. In *Sage Dictionary of Social Research Methods*. Ed. by Jupp, V. Oxford: Sage

Olwig, K. (1982) 'Education and the Sense of Place'. In *Geography and the Humanities*. Ed. by Cosgrove, D. Loughborough University of Technology: Loughborough, 38-53.

Ouseley, H. (2001) *Community Pride, Not Prejudice*. Bradford: Bradford Vision.

Outhwaite, W. (2017). (ed.) *Brexit: sociological responses*. London and New York: Anthem Press

Pahl, R. (1966) 'The Rural/Urban Continuum'. In *Readings in Urban Sociology*. Ed. by Anon. Oxford: Peragmom, 263-303.

Paxman, J. (1998). *The English: A Portrait of a People*. London: Penguin.

Philips, M. (2008) 'The Restructuring of Social Imaginations in Rural Geography'. *Journal of Rural Studies* 22, 113-122.

Philips, M. (2000) 'Theories of Positionality and Ethnography in the Rural'. In *Ethnography and Rural Research*. Ed. by Hughes, A., Morris, C., and Seymour, S. London: The Countryside and Community Press, 28-52.

Philo, C. (1992) 'Neglected Rural Geographies'. *Journal of Rural Studies* 8, 193-207.

Plastow, B. (2011) *Suppressing the Diversity of the 'Other': The Nature, Extent, and Impact of Racism Experienced by Visible Ethnic Minorities in Rural Scotland'*. PhD thesis or dissertation. Leicester University: Leicester.

Poole, D. (1997). *Vision, race and modernity: A visual economy of the Andean image world*. Princeton: Princeton University Press

Priestly, J. B. (1939) *Our Nation's Heritage*. London: Dent & Sons.

Punch, M. (1998) 'Politics and Ethics in Qualitative Research'. In The Landscape of Qualitative Research: theories and issues. Ed. by Denzin, N. K. and Lincoln, Y. S. California: Thousand Oaks, 156-184.

Putnam, R. (2000) *Bowling Alone: The Collapse and Revival of American Community*. New York: Simon and Schuster.

Ratner, C. (2002). 'Subjectivity and Objectivity in Qualitative Methodology'. *Qualitative Social Research* 3(3), 288-316.

Ray, L. and Reed, K. (2005) 'Community, Mobility, and Racism: Comparing Minority Experiences in East Kent'. *Journal of Ethnic and Racial Studies* 28 (2), 49-69.

Rees, A. (1950) *Life in a Welsh Countryside*. Cardiff: University of Wales Press.

Rex, J. and Mason, S. (eds.) (1986). *Theories of Race and Ethnic Relations*. Cambridge: Cambridge University Press

Rice, A. (2014). 'The gendered search to connect: Females and social media in rural Ireland'. In *The Internet and the Google Age*. Ed by. James, J. Dublin: Research Publishing, 51-61.

Richards, L. (1999). *Using NVivo in Qualitative Research*. London: Sage.

Richards, T. and Richards, L. (1998). 'Using Computers in Qualitative Research'. In *Collecting and Interpreting Qualitative Materials*. Ed. by Denzin, N. K. and Lincoln, Y. S. Thousand Oaks: Sage, 211-245.

Ritzer, G. (2000) *Modern Sociological Theory*. London: McGraw-Hill.

Ritzer, G. (1993) *The McDonaldisation of Society*. New York: Sage.

Robinson, V. and Gardner, H. (2004) 'Place Matters: Exploring the Distinctiveness of Racism in Rural Wales'. In *Rural Racism*. Ed. by Chakraborti, N. and Garland, J. London: Willan, 52-71

Rose, N. (2000) *The Politics of Life Itself: biomedicine, power and subjectivity in the Twenty-First Century*. Oxford: Oxford University Press.

Rose, N. (1999). 'The Death of the Social? Re-Figuring the Territory of Government'. In *Economy and Society*, 25 (3), 327-356.

Rowe, M. (2004) *Policing Race and Racism*. Willian: Cullompton.

Sarsby, J. (1997) 'From Cream Making to Coq Au Vin: Finding Images in Rural Devon'. In *Revealing Rural 'Others': Representation, Power, and Identity in the British Countryside*. Ed. by Millbourne, P. London: Pinter.

Savage, M.., Bagnall, G. and Longhurst, B. (2005). *Globalisation and Belonging*. London: Sage.

Scott, J. and Hogg, R. (2015) 'Strange and Stranger Ruralities: Social Construction of Community and Rural Crime'. *Journal of Rural Studies* 68 (1), 33-52.

Scruton, R. (2000) *England: An Elegy*. London: Chatto & Windus.

Scutt, R. and Bonnett, A. (1996) *In Search of England and Popular Representations of Englishness and the English Countryside*. Newcastle: Centre for Rural Economy.

Shaw, C and McKay, H. (1942). *Juvenile Delinquency and Urban Areas*. Chicago: University of Chicago Press.

Sheller, M. and Urry, J. (2004) *Event Mobilities: Places to Play, Places in Play'*. London: Routledge.

Shepland, J. and Vagg, J. (1988) *Policing by the Public*. London: Routledge.

Short, B. (1992) *The English Rural Community: Images and Analysis*. Cambridge: Cambridge University Press.

Shucksmith, M. (in press). 'Re-imaging the rural: from rural idyll to Good Countryside'. *Journal of Rural Studies* [online] http://www.sciencedirect.com/science/article/pii/S0743016716301632 (accessed 17 November 2016).

Shucksmith, M. (2010). 'Disintegrated Rural Development? Neo-endogenous rural development, planning and place shaping in diffused power contexts'. *Sociologia Ruralis*, 50 (1), 1-14.

Sibley, D. (1997) *Geographies of Exclusion: Society and Difference in the West*. London: Routledge.

Simmel, G. (1950) *The Sociology of Georg Simmel*. Glencoe: Free Press.

Skerratt, S. and Steiner, A. (2013). 'Working with communities-of-place: complexities of empowerment'. *Land Economy*, 28 (3), 320-338.

Soja, E. (1985) 'The Spatiality of Social Life: Towards a Transformative Re-theorisation'. In *Social Relations and Spatial Structure*. Ed. by Gregory, D. and Urry, J. London: Macmillan, 90-127

Stacey, M. and Pahl, R. (2006) 'The Myth of Community Studies'. *British Journal of Sociology* 57 (3), 134-147.

Stenson, K. (2005). 'Sovereignty, Bio-politics and the Local Governance of Crime in Britain.' *Theoretical Criminology*, 9 (3), 265–287

Stenson, K. and Edwards, A. (2004). 'Policy Transfer in Local Crime Control: Beyond Naive Emulation'. In *Criminal Justice and Political Cultures: National and International Dimensions of Crime Control*. Ed by. Newburn, T. and Sparks, R. Cullompton: Willan, 209-223.

Steventon, G. J. (2001) *Crime, Community, Context and Fear: Influences on Informal Social Control in an Affluent English Suburb*. Unpublished PhD thesis or dissertation. University of Warwick: Coventry.

Strathern, M. (1982) 'The Village as an Idea: Constructs of Village-Ness in Elmdon'. In *Belonging: Identity and Social Organisation in Rural Cultures*. Ed. by Cohen, A. P. London: Sage, 96-122.

Suttles, G. (1972) *The Social Construction of Communities*. Chicago: University of Chicago Press.

Taket, A. (2009) *Theorising Social Exclusion*. London: Routledge.

The Guardian (2016) 'Police Log Fivefold Rise in Race-Hate Complaints since Brexit Result'. The Guardian 30/06/2016.

The Guardian (2015). 'Farage's Muslim 'fifth column' remarks must not go unchallenged'. The Guardian 12/03/2015

The Independent (2013) 'A Rural Retreat near Stratford-upon-Avon: Not if You Build 4,500 Homes on it'. The Independent 22 August 2013.

Thrift, N. (2005) 'But Malice Aforethought: Cities and the Natural History of Hatred, Transaction of the Institute of British Geographers'. *Institute of British Geographers* 30, 130-150.

Tonnies, F. (1964) *Gemeinschaft Und Gesellschaft*. London: Harper.

Tucan, Y. F. (1980) 'Rootedness Versus Sense of Place'. *Landscapes* 24, 3-8.

Turner, V. (1974) *The Ritual Process*. London: Penguin.

Tyler, K. (2006) 'The Racialised and Classed Constitution of English Village Life'. *Journal of Anthropology* 68 (3), 391-412.

Urry, J. (2002). *The Tourist Gaze*. London: Sage.

Valentine, G. (2000) 'A Safe Place to Grow Up: Parenting, Perceptions of Children's Safety and the Rural Idyll'. *Journal of Rural Studies* 13, 137-148.

van Dijck, J. (2013). *The culture of connectivity: a critical history of social media*. Oxford: University of Oxford Press.

Vargaras-Silva, C. and Markaki, Y. (2015) *EU Rural Migration to the UK*. Oxford: Oxford Migration Observatory.

Videch, A., Bensman, K., and Stein, M. (1971) *Reflections on Community Studies*. New York: Harper.

Wallman, S. (1986) 'Ethnicity and the Boundary Process in Context'. *Theories of Race and Ethnicity* 26 (3), 12-30.

Ware, V. (2007). *Who cares about Britishness? A global view of the national identity debate*. London: Arcadia.

Wax, M. L. (1979). 'On the presentation of self in fieldwork: The dialectic of mutual deception and disclosure.' *Humanity & Society* 3, 248-259.

Weis, L., and Finn, M. (1994). *School choice and the struggle for the soul of American education*. New Haven: Yale University Press.

Williams, R. (1979) *The Country and the City*. London: Chatto and Windus.

Williams, W. M. (1956) *The Sociology of an English Village: Gosforth*. London: Routledge.

Wilson, J. and Kelling, G. (1982) 'Broken Windows: The Police and Community Safety'. *Atlantic Quarterly* (March), 29-38

Woldoff, R.; Lozzi, D. and Dilk, L. (2013), 'The social transformation of coffee houses: the emergence of chain establishments and the private nature of usage'. In *International Journal of Social Science Studies*, 1 (2), 205–218.

Woods, M. (2012). 'New directions in rural studies?'. *Journal of Rural Studies*, 28, 1– 4

Woods, M. (2007). 'Engaging the global countryside'. *Progress in Human Geography*, 31 (4), 495-507.

Woods, M. (2005). *Rural geography: processes, responses and experiences in rural restructuring*. London: Sage.

Woodruffe-Burton, H. (1998). 'Private desires, public display: consumption, postmodernism and fashion's 'modern man'. In *International Journal of Retail and Distribution Management*, 26, 301-310.

Wright, P. (2008) *On Living in an Old Country: The National Past in Contemporary Britain*. London: Verso.

Yarwood, R. and Gardner, G. (2000) 'Fear of Crime, Culture and the Countryside'. *Area* 40 (3), 4-11.

Yeoh, B. and Lau Wei Peng (1995) 'Historic District, Contemporary Meanings, Urban Conservation, and the Creation and Consumption of Landscape Spectacle in Tanjong Pager'. In *Portraits of Places: History, Community and Identity in Rural Singapore*. Ed. by Yeoh, B. and Kong, J. Singapore: Times Edition, 46-67.

Young, J. (2007) *The Vertigo of Late-Modernity*. Routledge: London.

Ziakas, V. and Boukas, N. (2013) 'Extracting Meaning from Events: A Phemonlogical Analysis of the Limassol Carnival'. *Journal of Destination Marketing and Management* 2 (2), 94-107.

Ziakas, V. and Costa, A. C. (2012) 'Between Theatre and Sport' in a Rural Event: Evolving Unity and Community Development from the Inside-Out'. *Journal of Sport and Tourism* 15 (1), 7-26.

Zorbaugh, W.H. (1929). *The Gold Coast and the Slum: A Sociological Study of Chicago's North Side*. Chicago: University of Chicago Press.

Zukin, S. (2010). *Naked City: The Death and Life of Authentic Urban Places*. Oxford: Oxford University Press.

An Ethnographic Excavation of the English Countryside:
A methodological appendix (A)

Introduction

In chapter 1 I outlined that an ethnography was conducted using semi-structured interviews, direct observations and participant observations. The purpose of this appendix is to enlarge upon the methodological process, with reference to why ethnography was chosen, how the methods were used and how the resultant data were analysed. I aim to demonstrate that ethnography was employed as a methodological strategy rather than as a method as part of a wider qualitative study. Ethnography as a qualitative method is typically regarded as a method of observation used to support and confirm other means of data collection (e.g., semi-structured interviews or surveys/questionnaires). However, as I go on to explain one of the key distinctions of ethnography as a methodological strategy as opposed to a qualitative method is that the approach incorporates the triangulation of data collection methods used within a broader ethnographic framework of reflexive practices of the researcher embedding themselves within the culture s/he is studying.

Under this context it is important, as Lois Weis and Michelle Finn (1994) argue, to provide reflexive accounts of the *'speed bumps'* that have happened whilst in the field. Speed bumps are unexpected moments in the research process when ethnographers reflect upon the practices and politics of ethnographic inquiry. As should be evident by now this book has documented many 'speed bumps', situations that have forced me to reflect on my own research agenda as well as my relationship with and responsibility to the rural community I was studying. Time and time again, my efforts at reciprocity forced me to think about my relationship with participants and the setting, necessitating a need to rearticulate the ethical complexities around issues of confidentiality and anonymity, the positionality of the researcher, and the constant luminal state of overt and covert participant observations.

Why ethnography?

Taking into account the nature and context of Brickington, I decided to use ethnography in conducting this piece of research. Ethnography is considered one of the central methodological approaches in qualitative research (Hammersley and Atkinson, 1995). Creswell (1998) defines ethnography as the social scientific study of culture through thick description and interpretation. Ethnographic research has a long and well-established history (Hughes and Morris, 2000); stemming from anthropology is the idea of the researcher going to faraway lands to study the social norms, practices, and habits of 'other' cultures. In more recent years ethnography has, as Jackson (1987: 10) puts it, 'come home', and social scientists are now applying ethnographic research to more everyday settings. Criminologists, sociologists, and geographers have taken advantage of ethnography, and the mid-twentieth century to the early twenty-first century saw interest in employing ethnographic techniques to rural settings (see for example, Taylor, 2006; Hetherington, 2006; Cloke, 1997; Bell, 1994; Newby, 1979; Videch *et al*, 1971; Williams, 1956; Rees, 1950).

However, ethnography is a complex term encompassing different, occasionally paradoxical meanings. Ethnography can be both a set of research methods (e.g., participant observation, semi-structured interviews), and a methodological approach (Hughes and Morris, 2000: 9) covering the methods used whilst in the field to the reflexivity of the researcher on the research process. The latter involves acknowledging the researcher's influence and impact on the research, and the role of their intentions, beliefs, and feelings have on the production of knowledge. Moreover, ethnography is informed by post-structural thinking: ethnographic research rejects objectivity and universal theories; instead, favouring conclusions which are drawn from the lived experiences of participants with the viewpoint that social realities are 'negotiated through, and shaped by, a kaleidoscope of social and cultural practices' (Hughes and Morris, 2000: 4).

Permeating studies of rural areas in sociology, criminology and human geography, ethnography has driven explorations and interpretations of the countryside. Most notably are the rural community studies undertaken from the 1950s to 1990s by the likes of Rees (1950), Williams (1956), Strathern (1982), and Bell (1994). Despite having different philosophical underpinnings than recent ethnographic studies of rural communities (see, for example, Taylor, 2006; Hetherington, 2006), they should not be dismissed as much can be learned from them (Hughes and Morris, 2000). Bell (1994), for instance, examined the impact of fieldwork on both the participants and the researcher, while Rees (1950) identified the need for rigorous procedures in obtaining 'trustworthy' data. The most important characteristic of these studies, nevertheless, was their attention to the mundane: successfully capturing complexity whilst guarding against over-generalised and sanitised accounts of everyday life.

Borrowing heavily from Bell and Newby's (1994) book, *Community Studies*, the return to 'dense' ethnography could be interpreted as a return to 'traditional' ethnography employed by early anthropologists (see, for example,

Malinowski, 1922 –reprinted in 2014; Benedict, 1946 – reprinted in 2014). This should not, nevertheless, blind us to the myopic return of ethnography: singular methods such as interviews and observations being passed as ethnography without consideration of the impact and influence of the researcher on the research process. This is what Cloke (1997: 369) has called a 'methodological swing from ethnography to ethnographic approaches'.

With different theoretical positions and interpretative lenses, ethnography has experienced a 'fractionalisation of meanings' (Phillips, 2000: 28); or in other words, there are multiple ways of defining ethnography signified by certain terms which have caused 'property disputes and conflicts' over how ethnography is used. Because of this ethnography has often become sealed in a 'hermeneutic quarantine of quotation marks' (Phillips, 2000: 28), denoting its contested and competing nature. Consequentially, ethnography is often a 'big tent' depicting a corpus of different approaches, clearly highlighting its nebulous nature that is subject to interpretation. For instance, Jackson (1994: 174) defines ethnography as 'first-hand observation...employing participant observation over other qualitative methods to convey the inner life and texture of a particular social group or neighbourhood', while Brewer (2000) suggests ethnography is much more than a set of methods and should include the influence and impact of the researcher in context.

Furthermore, in interrogating the presence of the researcher in context, ethnography must encompass in its definition a process of writing. Ethnographers must be committed to self-awareness that extends beyond tokenistic references to the partiality of being 'outside' or 'inside' the research setting. By favouring 'supplication, collaboration and empathy' (Phillips, 2000: 31) over control and explanation, ethnographers follow the post-structural task of 'establishing few stable coherences and situating life as played out in ebbs and flows' (Phillips, 2000: 31). This was pivotal in Bell's (1994: 243-244) ethnographic study of Childerley, where such considerations are evident throughout his time in the field in which by accepting his own vested interests would unavoidably creep into the mix, Bell managed to actualise his very presence in the social fabric of Childerly.

Discussing the importance of churches, trains and other symbols in facilitating his and his wife's daily lives in the village, Bell (1994) manages to immerse himself within the ever-changing context of Childerley. As Heley (2008: 24) observes, by 'standing at the margins, seeing life in part through the eyes of a Childerleyan, and in part through the eyes of one not fully enrolled, Bell felt well placed to trace the social complexities that constituted Childerly'.

The most important aspect of ethnography, therefore, is its commitment to 'seeing through the eyes of people being studied' (Bryman, 1988: 61) and for me this was the fundamental factor in choosing ethnography to study the maintenance and protection of Brickington's rural identity from wider social pressures of urbanisation, neoliberal expansion, and population growth. Not only did I need a methodology that could explore the constructed meanings of the lived experiences of residents of Brickington, but also how these understandings were framed in context, against the 'cultural backdrop' (Crotty, 1998: 7) of the residents doing the maintaining and protecting of local identity. Given that this is a study of complex social processes occurring in a specific setting, I felt as though the use of quantitative methods were not best appropriate. While surveys and questionnaires are useful in 'quantifying measurable facts' (Hollway and Jefferson, 2000: 2); they cannot comprehend why or how things occur or their constructed meaning. Thus, I do not dismiss the use of research methods, such as questionnaires, but I found these not to be the best way in accessing people's practical or tacit knowledge (Giddens, 1984; Altheide and Johnson, 1998). Consequentially, it was my belief that ethnography, through the use of diverse research strategies, could provide the means to access the tacit (Altheide and Johnson, 1998), practical (Giddens, 1984) and contextual understandings that quantitative methods might have failed to collect. It is these diverse research strategies in which I now turn to.

Data collection methods

Creswell (2003) describes ethnographic research as a strategy of exploration that occurs in a natural setting which enables the researcher to employ a triangulation of methods to gain an in-depth understanding of social life through actual lived experiences. In order to achieve this, Locke *et al.* (2004) maintain that ethnographers must consider the most appropriate methods of data collection to ensure relevant data is collected on the topic under investigation. In the following section, I provide an account and justification for each of the three components of my ethnographic strategy: semi-structured interviews, direct observations and participant observations.

Semi-structured interviews

From the outset, I knew I needed to conduct semi-structured interviews as one-third of my triangulation strategy as part of the wider ethnographic approach to the research. One of the key benefits of using semi-structured interviews to collect ethnographic data is the ethnographer's engagement in discussion and communication with residents of rural communities. By engaging in discussions the ethnographer can tap into how residents culturally construct the identities of where they live as being 'rural' by facilitating discourse embedded within their 'discursive consciousness' (Giddens, 1984), or in other words, the ability of residents to consciously and discursively construct the town's identity as 'rural'. Normally in qualitative research to test the applicability, feasibility and the requirements of a more detailed study, the researcher would set out to conduct a 'dummy-run' of the interview schedule being employed. The use of pilot interviews can be seen in Heley's (2008) ethnographic study of 'New Squierarchy'. Heley undertook an eight-week pilot study before the main study to establish some kind of objectivism of the questions being asked, as well as to consult with supervisors and colleagues to properly collate received data and develop interim conclusions with which to inform the future direction of his study. However, I find such an approach a bit of a red herring. If ethnography, as Philips (2000: 31) portrays it, is about understanding life as played out in 'ebbs and flows', then the application of pilot interviews is futile as the ethnographer would be interfering with the specific level of naturalness that would have come out of the data if he or she would have gone into the field 'blind'. It is for this reason why as part of the research process I decided against the use of pilot interviews: I aimed to achieve a certain level of naturalistic data that I would not have achieved if I had conducted pilot interviews.

This is not to say that my approach to collecting a certain level of naturalistic data is without its weaknesses. Because I decided to use a 'snowball' sampling method to recruit participants, there were limitations in terms of sample diversity. Since 'snowball' sampling is contingent on the social networks of participants (see Arber, 1993), I found this strategy not particularly useful in terms of recruiting minority ethnic residents of Brickington. This is because those who had initially shown interest in the study were mainly white, middle-class residents with local standing in the town that often passed onto me residents with similar class status and local standing. Even with the Polish and other minority ethnic participants I had managed to recruit through use of a local gatekeeper, Ellie; I still found the ethnic diversity of the sample not to be truly representative of the local community: a point made evident when examining the overall ethnic diversity of Brickington in comparison with the wider county (see Table 5.3).

In hindsight, because of the limitations in the diversity of the sample I could have employed an alternative sampling method, such as 'purposive' sampling, where recruitment of participants relies on the researcher making a judgement regarding which groups of people need targeting to obtain a representative sample of the community (Oliver and Jupp, 2006). However, I feel by purposefully considering alternative sampling strategies, the data collection process would have been too contrived and ergo competing with the epistemological nature of ethnography: that is, knowledge and understanding of communities should arise naturally through the course of doing the fieldwork, including the recruitment of participants for semi-structured interviews. The consequence of using such a naturalistic approach to recruitment meant I ended up with an overall sample size of 26 respondents (see Table A.1). While I had initial concerns regarding the sample size of the research, Braun, and Clarke (2013) reassured me that a sample size of 20+ respondents is perfectly suitable for a study of this size.

Table A.1 – List of Participants

Residents/age group	Born & bred	Moved from London	Polish	Other, from abroad
Rafael (20s)			√	
Jerzy (Teens)			√	
Joseph (60+)	√			
Irvin (60+)		√		
Barbara (60+)		√		
Julie (40s)	√			
Bobby (50s)	√	√		
Kris (50s)	√			
Steven (50s)				
Irene (60+)	√			
Jane (50s)	√			
Margaret (60+)	√			
Martha (60+)	√			
Deborah (40s)	√			
Susan (40s)	√			
Marc (40s)	√			
Donna (40s)	√			
Danielle (30s)	√			
Melissa (30s)	√			
Ann (60+)				√ Moved from Colombia
Faseeh (40s)				√ Moved from Mauritius
Marie & Rodney (65+ & 65+)				√ Moved from Germany and India
Helena & Ryan (40s & Teens)	√			
Kara (30s)			√	
Jake (20s)			√	
Dan (20s)			√	

Moreover, in conducting and carrying out the interviews, I decided in the early stages of my research and before the expedition to the setting to devise a basic schedule to use during the interview process (see Appendix B). My intention was to use 'progressive focusing' (Arksey and Knight, 1999: 18) where I first drew out some biographical data relating to the residents, such as history, length of residence in the area and what was good about Brickington or their motivation for moving to the town. In some interviews (e.g., Danielle, Deborah and Melissa, Faseeh, Irvin, and Marie), this background questioning led to dense biographical information. During the interviews with Faseeh, Irvin, and Marie I spent forty-five minutes discussing their backgrounds which led to detailed accounts of why and how they settled down in Brickington and their feelings towards the area.

Following background questioning the interviews were then formed around four broad themes: (i) an examination of a sense of community/sense of belonging, including what community life was like, participant's social networks and whether or not they felt attached to Brickington. (ii) An exploration of how residents perceived the urban/rural continuum of Brickington and whether this perception has changed over time. (iii) The types of local events/activities there are to do in Brickington and whether they took part or not, and if not, why? and (iv) an exploration of attitudes to and perceptions towards social change in Brickington. Within the parameters of these lines of enquiry, I intended to elicit information on a corpus of topics, including how residents related to and regarded their town as being 'rural' and the influence of wider social pressures on local life in the town.

My aim was to make the prescheduled questions as broad as possible (for example, what is life like in Brickington? or, how do you feel about the changes that have taken place in the town?) to not limit the direction the interviews took. Rather than myself beginning each discussion around fears of social change and the erosion of local identity, I intended for these topics/issues to arise naturally throughout the interview process. This meant that questioning about fear of change would not lead the direction of the interviews, but rather follow through other lines of enquiry. For example, in my interview with Kris discussions on fear of social change emerged early on when he began talking about how he felt towards the changes that had happened in Brickington over recent years whilst talking about his life history.

Getting contacts

My initial means of accessing residents was through 'snowball' sampling (Burgess, 1982). 'Snowball' sampling is the possibility of accessing residents where each person interviewed passed onto me another person (Burgess, 1982). My early engagement with the debates in the literature on identity and social change had suggested that people tend to be suspicious, and perhaps even fearful, of difference (see for instance Neal, 2009; Steventon, 2001). Thus, the advantages of 'snowball' sampling meant that it would minimise any distress or nervousness within my participants (Arksey and Knight, 1999). I had noticed a sense of apprehension on calling to arrange interviews with some of the residents in the setting. However, after identifying that their friend or colleague had put me in contact with them to see if they would be willing to conduct an interview for the study the majority expressed relief.

Moreover, 'snowball' sampling is largely dependent on the social network of people (Arber, 1993) whereby participants are in control of the researcher's access to further data. Out of the twenty-six residents interviewed, only seven residents were recruited using the 'snowball' method. The most imperative critique of 'snowball' sampling, therefore, is the selection process because contacts are only given within limited social networks (Arber, 1993) and dependent on people's busy lives with other priorities used as an excuse to decline. For instance, the contacts given by my then sister-in-law offered little in terms of the geographical spread of Brickington; they seemed to focus on colleagues with whom she worked or had worked with. I managed to get into contact with three members of the Polish community through my then sister-in-law, but they were hesitant and did not fully understand the purpose of the interview until I arrived for it.

An Alternative Approach

'Snowball' sampling offered little in the way of recruiting participants, thus I needed another means of accessing the residents of Brickington. After interviewing Jane, she was able to put me in contact with Ellie. But despite the purpose of the contact being to conduct another interview; Ellie had thought Jane wanted her to help me in the recruitment process. Ellie was a social care practitioner who also lectured in community studies at a university in the south of England and was keen on helping me find future participants for the study. Such a relationship can have consequences for research in which the gatekeeper can 'shape the conduct and development of the research' (Hammersley and Atkinson, 1995: 75) by promoting their own agenda. However, the ethical problems around using 'gatekeepers' as an entry point into the research setting was not a large conundrum for me. Ellie was not a 'gatekeeper' in the sense of the word as I did not have to rely on her for access to the field site, but she was in the sense of helping me in the recruitment process. In the end, this proved to be a fruitful endeavour in getting contacts as she put me in touch with seven further participants. However, I was aware of the consequences that given contacts likely came from her own social world and therefore might have recruited similar people with similar views; ergo jeopardising the diversity of the sample of participants within the setting.

Direct observations

As a second component of my ethnographic strategy, I employed one to four-hour direct observations during the day and evening including all days of the week. The advantage of using direct observations is that it provides a record of the behaviours that occurred naturally. Ethnographers do not have to ask what they would do or what they would think: they have a record of the everyday, routine actions of people (Ary *et al.*, 2013). In all, I conducted one-month worth of direct observations averaging three hours a day to passively observing the daily lives of the residents of Brickington. The direct observations were recorded using either a Dictaphone or written directly into a field diary. All of which was then written up into a Microsoft Word document after the fieldwork to allow the data to be easily imported into NVivo for analysis.

With regard to the details of the direct observations, I would walk along street frontages and the High Street, take a trip to the local shops or sit on a bench or in local cafes for a few hours, ordering mug after mug of coffee undertaking observational research. Like Bell (1994), I found myself observing residents engaging in a range of everyday activities. These included conversations amongst residents who knew each other, to casual encounters on the High Street (e.g., saying 'morning' or 'hi' as a customary nicety), to the types of peoples who would use specific shops.

I made use of a field diary to jot down long passages of conversation and routine activities of residents. These jottings of routine activities and conversations between residents were useful because whilst writing about these events I could present thick descriptive accounts of the everyday goings-on of the residents of Brickington (see Chapter 6). For where those shorter conversations and routine activities occurred, however, in spaces such as the High Street, on street frontages and around shops I found myself having to use my 'mental Dictaphone' (Bell 1994: 247) and jot down the observations later that day from memory. While apprehensive, at first, about applying such an approach to record my observations, I acknowledged that these situations might have arisen because of wanting to obtain a defensive level of naturalness about the data. Nevertheless, these situations are not unusual in ethnographic studies as such incidents were evocative of Bell's (1994: 247) fieldwork in Childerley: 'I had to say things intended for the mental Dictaphone when the mechanical one was off or at home'.

Although direct observations allowed me to capture conversations and everyday habits of the Brickington community and its residents, they were also imperative in the interpretation of what people said about the way they engage socially (Shapland and Vagg, 1988). In my interview with Barbara, she felt that security was a crucial part of rural life in the town and that 'neighbours watching out for one another' was an important part of this sense of security: 'On this street we are the nosiest group of people you'll know so if someone different moved in we would know about it'. However, during my hour-long observation along the street frontage where she lived, I noticed a young couple moving into their new house. On questioning Barbara about whether any new residents had moved onto the street, she said 'I know everybody on the street. The last person to move to Sheen Way was Pat and Carl twenty years ago'. This highlights some of the contradictory and messy ways between what people say they know and what people actually know.

While portraying the use of direct observation as problem-free, there are limitations involved in conducting them. For instance, DeWalt and DeWalt (1998) advocate that, while direct observations capture a snapshot of community actions and practices they do not provide explanations for why those community actions and practices occur in the first instance. This has led Ratner (2002) to conclude that, in order provide any meaningful understanding of community or cultural life; ethnographers need to employ multiple observational methods to ensure that what he/she observes is, in fact, a representative depiction of community life. Because of this, I decided to employ participant observations during the fieldwork also as part of my ethnographic triangulation strategy.

Participant observations

Breuer and Roth (2003) maintain that one of the most important methods of data collection within an ethnographic study is participant observations. Participant observations are crucial for the ethnographer to experience the culture of his or her research context as it often leads to a richer understanding of the research context and the participants. The use of participant observations had a clear advantage for this study. They allowed me to access, what Goffman (1999 - originally published in 1959) called the 'backstage culture' of rural life in Brickington and offered a chance for a thick descriptive account of local events. In other words, I was able to place myself more fully into the spaces and culture of Brickington by recording local practices and engagements from within the community.

Participant observations were employed and conducted at various times and places throughout the fieldwork: specifically, when local events and activities were happening and often lasted between one to five hours. One event in which participant observations were conducted was during the local Brickington carnival (see Chapter 5). These observations involved being part of the crowd watching the procession and partaking in local life by engaging in funfair activities and talking to local stall sellers. Reminiscent of Bell's (1994) study where he was invited to dinner parties and evenings down the pub from local residents he had interviewed, I experienced a comparable situation. During a casual stroll around the funfair grounds, I bumped into Bobby I had known from conducting the interviews. During the conversation, I mentioned that I was trying to embed myself into the local community of Brickington to understand the importance of local events on the local identity of the place. From here, Bobby invited me to sit in on one of the local carnival committee meetings to gain insight into the running and organisation of the event (see Chapter 5). Other events where participant observations were conducted included St. Peters craft fair and market and while on the High Street (see Chapter 6). Like the carnival, my observations involved participating in the local life of the event by talking to stall sellers/shop owners and purchasing local produce.

Unlike the direct observations that were primarily captured using either a Dictaphone or a field diary, participant observations were normally recorded from memory. This is because I thought the obvious presence of a Dictaphone or field diary in my hands would have made residents ill at ease. Following Bell's (1994: 247) example, therefore, I 'tried to ensure that topics were remembered ... however various the social situation...while at the same time providing space for other conversational ground that the residents thought significant'. However, for those occasions, such as watching the carnival procession, where I blended in with the rest of the community I jotted down notes on themes and interactions I had seen into my field diary.

The use of triangulation between participant observations and other means of data collection (e.g., semi-structured interviews and direct observations) added depth to the study in terms of analysis, which often reflected how residents of Brickington constructed the town's identity as 'rural'. By involving formal and informal corroboration, using a range of methods, this study - like most ethnographies – provided a more holistic approach to data collection; not only with regards to the collection of information and its use in the field (capturing residents' discursive and practical consciousness), but also in relaying it to a wider audience (e.g., the writing of this book).

Reflexivity: my presence as an 'outsider'

Reflexivity was an important part of my research. The concept and practice of reflexivity has been described as the 'interpretation of interpretation' (Denzin and Lincoln, 2000: 17) where ethnographers need to be aware of their effect on the research process as 'knowledge cannot be separated from the knower and that, within the social sciences, there is only interpretation, nothing speaks for itself' (Denzin and Lincoln, 2000: 17). Therefore, it is impossible for the ethnographer to be fully 'outside' the subject matter; his or her presence, in whatever form, will have some kind of effect. It is through the depiction of the researcher's account of the research process that s/he will be able to offer a plausible understanding of the research setting and the effect to which s/he has had on it.

For this particular study, being a white, middle-class researcher occasionally put me in the disadvantageous position of not sharing similar characteristics with the minority ethnic residents I interviewed. Having a different marker of identity can produce obvious barriers in the researcher-participant relationship. Such a barrier was acknowledged by Duneier (2005) in his research on racism in New York. He found that although there was a strong unifying factor, racially, between himself and his interviewees, there were still differences in terms of social class, educational background, and occupation. Similarly, coming from Coventry allowed me to have a shared (geographical) identity with some of the participants in which I was able to share with them feelings of anxiety and 'not-belonging' within Brickington's rural 'idyll'.

By the same token, many residents were not afraid to express their opinions regarding other residents, in particularly Polish residents, who had moved into the area: opinions that probably would not have been expressed if it were not for my white, middle-class background. Nevertheless, I found myself consistently questioning my position as an 'outsider' throughout the research process. As a researcher with my background, I found myself often asking would it be any more legitimate for me to interview individuals who were of a shared 'racial' background? Or, would my 'outsider' status override my identity as a white heterosexual male when it came to interviewing longer-term residents of Brickington? In the end, my ability to cross identity boundaries allowed me to identify and establish contact with both.

Furthermore, the residents' fear of change/difference was also difficult to determine from observations, especially considering the reactions I received as an outside researcher during the craft fair (see Chapter 6). While concerns about me as an 'outsider' (and particularly an 'urban outsider' from Coventry) were expressed by one gentleman I had called to arrange an interview when he began interrogating me on the nature of the study and whether or not I had ever been to Brickington, my presence did not give rise to too many confrontations. This is not to say that I was never noticed during my observations. Many of my observations were conducted on foot, and it was difficult to maintain incognito in areas of Brickington which were exceptionally quiet. The absence of life along one street frontage one afternoon in October 2013 made my presence aware of one gentleman mowing his lawn to which he kindly asked if I was lost. On being noticed, I decided to cut the observation short.

Evidently, the data that came out of interviews which suggested a fear of difference/change - a theme that I have developed throughout this book was contradictory to the apparent disregard of my presence as an 'outsider' as well as what has been suggested in the literature (see Neal, 2009). Perhaps the reason for this is that as rural towns and villages grow and people are more readily able to access rural environments the boundaries of who does and who does not belong become blurred. Steventon's (2001: 275-276) study of an affluent Midlands suburb describes an analogous situation where despite one gentleman saying that outsiders were monitored by the residents of the suburb his presence went largely unnoticed.

Clearly then, this dichotomy of an apparent disregard of my presence as an 'outsider' and residents sense of fear of change/fear of difference highlighted in the interview data throughout this book describe the paradoxical character of rural life: that is, despite residents' perceptions of Brickington as a 'rural community' with strong, close-knit social networks, residents are generally unaware of who is and who is not an 'outsider'. Perhaps a point of concern which has been co-opted by long-term residents into their practical and discursive resistances towards widening patterns of social change happening in the local area?

Data analysis: working with NVivo

Ethnographic data can be very voluminous and complex (Richards and Richards, 1998). Qualitative data packages can be useful, in this regard, as they can help researchers organise and analyse unstructured data. Software packages allow researchers to arrange and sort information; explore relationships and patterns in the data; and combine analysis through shaping, modelling, and linking data. For this study, I decided to use NVivo for its capabilities of coding and analysis and generating theory.

Ethnographers usually develop theoretical ideas by applying an abductive approach where they work 'up' from the data and work 'down' from existing theory (Richards and Richards, 1998: 213). Taking an abductive approach means drawing upon knowledge found within the literature while also creating knowledge out of the data which, in turn, reprioritises and reshapes the literature the researcher draws upon (Richards, 1999: 213). Categorisation of my research data took three forms: descriptive (description of geographical location, sense of place and participants of the study); concepts derived from the literature (community, built environment, social change, difference, informal social control and identity); and issues drawn out of the data (safety, security and protection, class, threat and belonging, exclusion and racism). Within NVivo data can be structured into hierarchical tree nodes, and the issues derived from my research and distinguished from existing theory lent themselves to a clear hierarchical development (see Figure A.1).

Figure A.1 – Hierarchical tree coding in NVivo

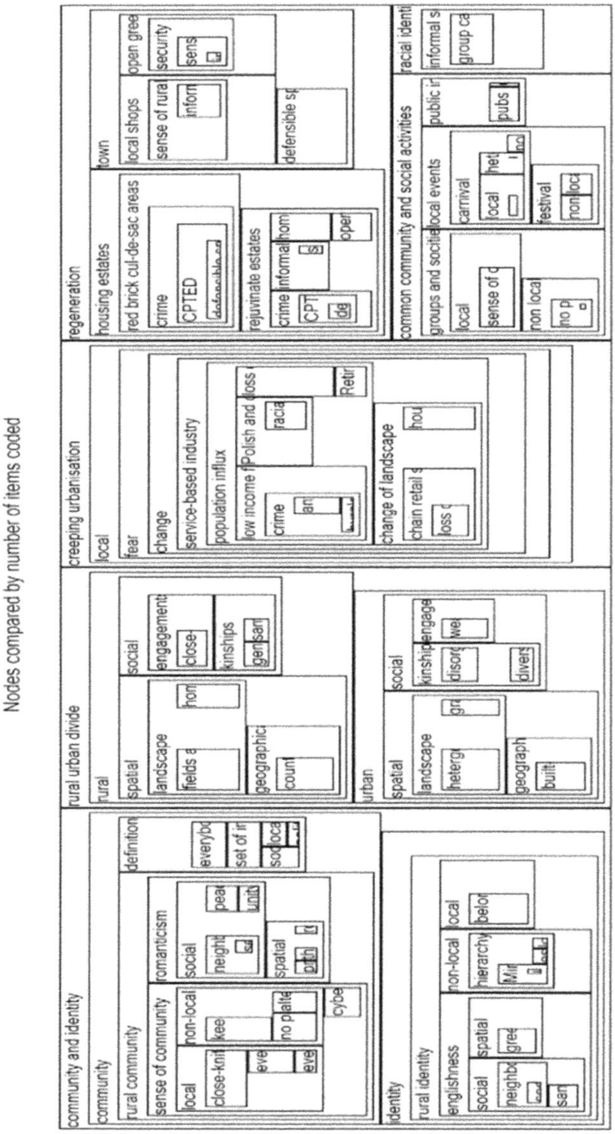

Despite depicting my analytical process as straightforward, it was, in fact, complicated and messy. I experienced a problem, not because of the complexity of data *per se* but the lack of sufficiently knowing the data; to put it simply the use of NVivo took away my agency as the researcher. Crowley *et al.* (2002) maintain despite the advantages of robustness in data analysis programs such as NVivo, they often leave the researcher feeling 'out of control' as the software can neatly organise data into appropriate codes without having to 'get to know your data'. This was a central problem for me when I came to analyse and code my data. Because NVivo allowed me to transcribe and code single sections into the themes that I had drawn out of the data I often found myself not having to reread sections of the transcriptions but simply retrieve the lines I needed from the node it was placed. However, I do not think this was necessarily the fault of NVivo itself, but rather how I used it. I often found myself coding lines of single text into their specific nodes so when trying to examine the 'wholeness' of the data I struggled to identify which of its constituted parts were relevant to my overall analysis.

For this reason, I adopted an alternative approach to analysing the data, which involved re-reading typed transcripts and field notes, and making connections between the data in a standard Microsoft Word document, using thematic analysis (Braun and Clarke, 2006). Coding was conducted using 'track changes'. This included highlighting text (e.g., phrases and words) which were considered important to the overarching aims and objectives of the research. From here superordinate themes were drawn based on key concepts taken from the literature (e.g., identity, community, difference, informal social control, social change), and concepts which arose naturally from other lines of enquiry (e.g., exclusion, racism, class, threat, belonging, security). Such an approach provided an overall wholeness, which I could not achieve from NVivo.

Ethical dilemmas

Confidentiality and anonymity

Issues of anonymity and confidentiality were important in this study as my aim was to explore the influence of informal social control on protecting local identity in a specific rural setting and so was aware that the people I interviewed may have disclosed information about their social lives and feelings about Brickington/people in Brickington which they may not want other residents to know. The maps and diagrams used in this book have also been suitably disguised to protect the identity of the place and copyright permission was sought and given.

Despite this, the idea of absolute confidentiality and anonymity is implausible (Christians, 2000; Kidd and Judd, 1986). Pseudonyms may disguise locations to those situated outside of the research setting but are often recognised by those living within the town (Christians, 2000; Punch, 1998), and because of the type of research setting the thick description derived from my observations make this more likely. The alteration of details could also affect contextual nature of ethnography and make its application futile.

One solution to overcoming this dilemma is to adopt a certain level of professionalism; that is, the researcher's specific duty of care to the participants s/he is studying in order that no harm, embarrassment, or insensitivity is endured to them during the fieldwork. Fielding (1993) expresses that it is impossible to predict the ethical repercussions of fieldwork and therefore it becomes a balancing act where, as researchers, ethnographers need to weigh up potential harm alongside what contributions to knowledge (Kidd and Judd, 1986) the research will make. My research paints a timely picture of a rural community, and thus, since places are changeable and porous (Massey, 1994), the setting is likely to change over time inevitably and any potential emotional and psychological effects on those involved will disappear as people's lives change and alter.

Insider and outsider perspectives

Another ethical dilemma that I had to consider was my position as outsider researcher, as opposed to an insider researcher, to the claims made about the experiences of local life and its impact on the trustworthiness of the data collected. Insider research is research conducted with populations of which the researcher is also a member (Kanuha, 2000). The researcher shares an identity and cultural base with the participants being studied (Asselin, 2003). Scholars such as Adler and Adler (1987) suggest an 'insider' status gives ethnographers a certain amount of legitimacy in which participants are more likely to be open so that there may be a greater defensible level of credibility to the data gathered.

In Adler and Adler's (1987) work of 'insider' researchers, they also assert that the role of an 'insider' can result in greater level of trust and openness to the research that may maintain a decent level of confirmability (see also, Brannick and Coghlan, 2007; Asselin, 2003) contrast to that of the 'outsider perspective' where participants are less likely to willing to allow access because there is a stigma: 'it is as if they feel, you are one of them, and it is us versus them (those on the outside don't understand)' (Asselin, 2003: 70).

Despite insider research being advantageous as it allows access and entry, it does nevertheless obfuscate the research process. The 'insider's' perceptions might be based on assumptions of his or her personal bias as a member of the community which he or she may have difficulty distancing themselves from. In this regard, I find my status as an 'outsider' to have resulted in greater confirmability of the data collected. Even though there were chances of taking my own a priori knowledge about the research to the setting, it was not possible for me to cloud the research with my own personal experiences as I was not a resident of Brickington: thus, maintaining a defensible level of trustworthiness.

Overt or covert participant observations

It has long been acknowledged that, when conducting ethnographic research within communities, ethnographers may have to tailor data collection methods to collect appropriate data (Goffman, 1963; Hobbs, 2002; Lee, 1993). This is because ethnographic research is naturalistic, meaning the researcher does not intervene in the activities of the people being studied (Adler and Adler, 2000). The use of certain data collection methods used in ethnographic research, therefore, need to be put under ethical scrutiny.

As an ethnographic field method that allows researchers to observe what people do in their natural contexts, participant observations can supply detailed, authentic information unattainable by other research methods (Homan, 1980; Humphreys, 1970; Gans, 1999), such as semi-structured interviews or direct observations. Ethnographic participant observations could be overt or covert, with or without revealing the purpose of the study. Although covert participant observations are more likely to provide detailed portraits of contextualised social realities, its use has stirred much controversy and debate around research ethics, mainly regarding deception and the absence of informed consent from the people being studied (Bulmer, 1982; Dingwall, 1980; Wax, 1979).

In response to these ethical concerns regarding participant observations, ethnographers are advised to conduct participant observation overtly and openly in which the researcher is obliged to make note s/he is conducting research when engaging in conversation with the local people of the community under study. Nevertheless, because the ethnographer is living alongside members of the host community, participating in events, work, leisure activities and hanging out, those same community members will not be fully aware that the ethnographer will faithfully record accounts of these events as soon as possible and that this will form part of the data analysis (DeWalt and DeWalt, 2002). In fact, community members rarely give explicit informed consent while engaged in casual conversation during trips to local shops, or while purchasing something at a craft fair or participating in local events and activities. Indeed, if participants were consciously aware of our activities as ethnographers the information acquired would be less rich (DeMunck and Sobo, 1998) and naturalistic.

For this reason, Lugosi (2006) argues that the use of participant observations in ethnographic research is always going to be in a luminal state between overt or covert research. Punch (1998: 10) claims, therefore, that participant observations are not inherently unethical: 'by virtue, they are intentionally deceitful'. That is, participant observations are by nature deceptive, and so it may be necessary, on occasion, to not disclose your true intentions in order to achieve a credible level of naturalness about the data as participants may alter their behaviour and what they say to fit the purpose of the research. It is because of this that ethnographers should characterise participant observations as ethically challenging and present a reflexive account of such issues, rather than suggesting participant observations are intrinsically unethical.

My participant observations of the local craft fair and market at St. Peters church provided me with this exact dilemma. Whilst looking around I stopped to purchase some marmalade and cakes to take back to my then in-laws who were housing me during the fieldwork. On purchasing the product, I started to engage in conversation with the elderly stall seller. She highlighted some of the niceties of the fair and market, such as some of the community coming together to celebrate the local area and create a sense of rural identity. She was very proud of the fact that 'local people were selling local products to local people'. She conferred to me that events like the craft fair and market are important to the Brickington community as it acted as a retreat from, what she deemed the 'ugliness' of the town since bigger businesses had arrived. At this moment in the conversation, I could have indicated that I was a researcher from Coventry University who was studying how Brickington constructed rural life amid the backdrop of such changes. However, by not disclosing my position I managed to elicit some rich contextual data from the participant observation of the craft fair and market about how local events are used in reproducing local identity - something which I may not have achieved had I been completely honest about my research (see Chapter 6 for a more detailed account of my participant observations at the St Peters craft fair and market).

Interview Schedule (Appendix B)

Opening

A. (*Establish Rapport*) [shake hands] My name is Nathan Kerrigan and I am from Coventry University

B. *(Purpose)* I would like to ask you some questions about your community, the activities you would normally partake in and around the town and general attitudes towards the area you live.

C. (*Motivation)* The aim of the interview is to collect data on the way residents interact with their community and the attitudes they have towards it. This will then, with your informed consent, be collected and analysed for my doctorate research.

D. (*Time Line*) The interview should take between 45-90 minutes. Are you okay with that?

(**Transition**: Let me begin by asking you some questions about yourself, where you live and its residents)

Body

A. (Topic) General Biographic/Demographic Information

1. Tell me a little about yourself.
    a. How long have you lived in Brickington?
    b. What attracts/attracted you to Brickington?
2. What is life like in Brickington?
    a. In what ways has life changed in Brickington?
        i. What is different about Brickington?
        ii. What factors contribute to making Brickington feel different?
        iii. What is the main difference in Brickington?
    b. So, life has stayed pretty much the same. Why is this?
        i. Why is it that life in Brickington has stayed the same?
        ii. What factors make life in Brickington continuous and unchangeable?

        iii. Can you explain why Brickington feels the same or unchanged?

3. What types of people would you say live in Brickington? Has the social mix changed at all?

    a. Why has the social mix changed?

        i. What factors have contributed to the change in the types of people who live in Brickington?

        ii. Does the change in Brickington's social mix affect the town's cultural identity?

        iii. **(Optional)** Has crime increased in Brickington?

    iii(a) In what ways has crime increased?

    b. Why has not the social mix changed

        i. What factors contribute to the consistency of Brickington's population?

        ii. Why is it that the social mix in Brickington has not changed?

B. *(Topic) Sense of Belonging/Sense of Community*

1. What is the community like in Brickington?

    a. Why is Brickington's community so close-knit?

        i. Explain the factors that contribute to this close-knittedness?

        ii. Does this idea of close-knittedness provide of a sense of security?

    b. Why is Brickington's community so detached?

        i. Explain the factors that contribute to this distance?

    c. What impact does this have on the identity of the town?

2. What does community mean to you?

    a. Why is belonging and closeness important to this notion of community?

    b. In what ways does Brickington reflect your idea of community?

        i. How does it reflect your idea of community? Explain the reasons why?

        ii. Why does not it? Explain the reason for why this is?

3. Has the sense of community changed over the years?
   a. How has Brickington's sense of community changed?
      i. Explain the factors that have contributed to this?
   b. Why has not Brickington's sense of community changed?
      i. Explain why this is?

4. What are the social engagements like in Brickington?
   a. Are they close-knit?
      i. Why are such engagements important to the community in Brickington?
      ii. Do they reflect your notion of community?
   b. Are they distant?
      i. Why is this?
      ii. What factors have contributed to this?

C. (Topic) Common Community and Social Activities

1. What sorts of activities/events are there to do in Brickington?
   a. Are these activities/events common in Brickington?
   b. Do they reflect the social engagements that exist in Brickington?

2. Would you say these activities/events are important to the community?
   a. Do such activities/events promote a sense of community?
      i. What are the reasons for this?
      ii. What are reasons for they do not?

3. Would you normally partake in any of these activities/events?
   a. What are your feelings to interacting in such activities/events
      i. Do you achieve a sense of belongings from such events/activities?
   b. What do not you contribute to these events?
      i. Is there a lack of belonging for why this is?

D. (Topic) Rural/Urban Divide

1. What type of town would you say Brickington is? Is it rural or urban?

  a. How would you define rural?

    i. What factors contribute to Brickington being perceived as 'rural'?

    ii. What ways of doing and living would you describe as rural and how does this reflect Brickington?

    iii. **(Optional)** Does this sense of rurality impact on this idea of security?

 a(i) Alternatively the, how would you define urban?

  b. What factors contribute to Brickington perceived as 'urban'?

    i. What ways of doing and living would you describe as 'urban' and how does this reflect Brickington?

2. What impact does this have on the identity of Brickington?

  a. Does this notion of rural reflect with feelings of Englishness and community

    i. What elements of Brickington reflect this?

  b. How does this notion of urban reflect feelings of Englishness and community in Brickington?

    i. What elements of Brickington reflect this?

3. Does this affect the cultural makeup of Brickington?

  a. In what ways has this affected the cultural makeup of Brickington?

  b. Explain the factors that contribute to the difference in Brickington's cultural identity?

E. *(Topic) Impacts of Urbanisation*

1. Does the increase in service-based shops affect this notion of 'Englishness' in Brickington?

  a. What ways have service-based shops have affected this notion of 'Englishness' in Brickington?

  b. Does the increase in service-based industry decrease Brickington's sense of community?

2. Do these service-based shops have an impact on Brickington's cultural identity

  a. How would you perceive Brickington's cultural identity with the increase of service-based shops?

      b.   Have service-based shops made Brickington's cultural identity more distant?

  3.   Do the service-based shops affect the view, or design of Brickington?

      a.   Has the landscape of Brickington changed with the rise of service-based shops?

      b.   In what ways has Brickington's landscape changed?

      c.   Does this impact on the sense of belonging?

(**Transition:** Well, it has been a pleasure finding out more about you. Let me briefly summarize the information that I have recorded during our interview....

Closing

A. (*Summarize*) Summary of the questions given and what has been discussed.

B. (*Maintain Rapport*) I appreciate the time you took for this interview. Is there anything else you would like to add before I finish?

C. (*Action to be taken*) I should have all the information I need. Contact me if you would like for your interview to be withdrawn from the research. My contact details are on the participant information sheet. Thanks again.

Index

A

Aberystwyth, 149
ability/lack, 61
Abingdon, 149
Abrams, 121, 143
Academic Press, 144
academics, 38, 62
accentuates, 33
acceptance, 120, 126
  conditional, 127
accessing people, 162
accoutrements, 22
accusations, 55
acknowledgement, 45
  unpanicked, 96
acquired colonial wealth, 27
actions
  oft-repeated, 82
  people's, 141
  practical, 63
  routine, 167
actions people, 84
  practical, 59
actions resonate, 56
actions/routines, 7
active form, 113
activities
  based social, 126
  event's, 89
  funfair, 89

  local, 137
  place-based, 90
activities/events, 179
acts, 20, 23, 28, 51, 53, 55–56, 58, 75, 83, 87, 112, 124, 133
  rural village, 127
  stable state system, 133
actualising, 2, 48
acute people, 1
adhering, 56, 102
Adler, 143, 174–75
Adult World, 151
Advocacy, 149
affair, small, 101
affections, 15–16
affirmation, 83
affluent, 40, 45, 54, 99
Affluent English Suburb, 155
affluent identity, 99
affluent newcomers, 119
affluent wealthy, 127
afraid and anxious individuals, 122
age, 40, 67, 140, 146
  digital, 41
  golden, 47
a gem, 70
agencies, 34, 62, 173
agenda, 137, 166
  better policy, 140
  multiculturalist, 24
Aggregate-level Analysis, 149
aggression, 18, 41

C

J

W

Lightning Source UK Ltd.
Milton Keynes UK
UKHW031251111120
373211UK00010B/612/J